Go Ye...
and Teach

Go Ye...
and Teach

by

RALPH COTTRELL

BAKER BOOK HOUSE
Grand Rapids, Michigan

Copyright © 1971 by Baker Book House Company

ISBN: 0-8010-2325-4

Library of Congress Catalog Card Number: 79-172298

Printed in the United States of America

To my devoted wife

Mary Lee

and our children

Sherry, Evelyn, and *David*

this book is affectionately

dedicated.

FOREWORD

Careful observation of numerous teaching situations in various local churches over the past twenty-five years has led me to the conclusion that one of the greatest needs of the teaching ministry of today is encouragement and inspiration for the individual teacher. As with no other individual or group in the church, the efforts and the contributions of the dedicated teacher are largely unrecognized and, as a logical result, unappreciated by both the leadership and the church membership in general.

While it is recognized that organization is most surely essential to the attainment of an effective teaching ministry in the church, it should be remembered that the best organization cannot reach peak efficiency unless those who are involved in that organization also reach peak efficiency. It appears that the attention focused on the perfecting of the organization may have, in some instances, overshadowed the attention and energy devoted to securing, training, and encouraging the people most involved in the teaching ministry — the individual teachers. When the final analysis has been made, it will be revealed that the individual teacher is the key to effective teaching! For this very good reason, it is believed that attention must be centered on the individual teacher and a renewed interest must be shown in him as a teacher.

This book makes no effort to deal with the mechanics of teaching. It is intended simply and solely as an effort to offer encouragement and inspiration to those men and women who have dedicated themselves to the work of teaching the Word of the Lord in the local church.

In recognition of and appreciation for these many dedicated teachers who often labor under adverse circumstances this book has been written. It is the prayer of the author that the contents of this book will be used of the Lord to both encourage and inspire the Christian teachers of this age to attain greater teaching efficiency.

Ralph Cottrell

Texarkana, Arkansas

CONTENTS

Foreword	7
1. The Teacher	11
2. The Challenge	31
3. Motivation	47
4. Consecration	79
5. Preparation	99
6. Presentation	119

1
THE TEACHER

THE MINISTRY OF THE TEACHER
HAS BEEN PLACED ON A PLANE
OF EQUAL IMPORTANCE
WITH THAT OF THE APOSTLES,
THE PROPHETS, THE EVANGELISTS,
AND THE PASTOR.

1

THE TEACHER

And he gave some, apostles; and some, prophets; and some, evangelists; and some, pastors and teachers; For the perfecting of the saints, for the work of the ministry, for the edifying of the body of Christ: Till we all come in the unity of the faith, and of the knowledge of the Son of God, unto a perfect man, unto the measure of the stature of the fullness of Christ: That we henceforth be no more children, tossed to and fro, and carried about with every wind of doctrine, by the sleight of men, and cunning craftiness, whereby they lie in wait to deceive; But speaking the truth in love, may grow up into him in all things, which is the head, even Christ (Ephesians 4:11-15).

I. The Illustrious Companions of the Teacher

The teacher is by no means alone in his efforts to advance the kingdom of God. Ephesians 4:11-14, as no other passage of Scripture, sets before us the majesty and order of the ministry of the church. Listen to the divine roll call of those charged with the awesome responsibility of teaching in the church.

A. Apostles

And he gave some, apostles. . . .

An apostle is an official representative, or ambassador, of the Lord. Christ chose His apostles and sent them forth for the purpose of representing Him among men. These were the earliest *official* or *ordained* representatives of the Lord, and this passage of Scripture reminds us that the teacher in the church of today has a most definite relationship to those representatives. There is an important link in the chain of Scriptural teaching, extending from the days of our Lord on earth to this present day. The teacher in the church classroom today will gratefully acknowledge the fact that he is singularly blessed in having the privilege of continuing the work begun by the early apostles of the Lord.

B. Prophets

. . . and some, prophets. . . .

In addition to the apostles the Lord gave to the church some prophets. Prophets are the inspired messengers of the Lord. Who were they? In view of the fact that a prophet is both a "foreteller" and a "forthteller," it is evident that those "holy men of God" who "spake as they were moved by the Holy Ghost" were the writers of the Old Testament. Certainly the writers of the New Testament qualify for this distinction as they both *wrote* and *spoke* under direct inspiration of the Lord. The teacher of the Word of the Lord most certainly is identified with the prophets for

. . . he gave some, prophets . . . and teachers.

This indicates that both prophets and teachers were given to the church by the Lord.

C. Evangelists

. . . and he gave . . . some, evangelists. . . .

THE TEACHER

To the illustrious apostles and prophets who were given of the Lord to the church we now find added that most important person—the evangelist. An evangelist is the announcer of good news. In the plan of the Lord for the proclamation of His Word He included what has become known today as the preacher. The evangelist was placed in the church by the Lord to announce the Good News about Jesus and His relationship with man. From the days of Christ's earthly ministry to the present time, the church has had among her official workers the evangelist or teller of the Good News to the masses. The teacher is identified with the evangelist in the overall task of the church.

D. Pastors

> *. . . and he gave . . . some, pastors. . . .*

Apostles, prophets, and evangelists have been set in the church for their particular work. To these the pastor has been added that he may aid them in their field of labor. Perhaps there is some confusion in the minds of some as to the real work of the pastor. As has been noted, many feel that the pastor is just a preacher or, in a sense, an evangelist. It is noteworthy that pastors and evangelists are set in the church as two distinct personalities. The primary work of the evangelist is to *proclaim the Good News* (preach); while the primary function of the pastor is to *shepherd the flock*. A shepherd watches over the flock and protects them from harm. It is the work of the pastor to watch over the spiritual welfare of his congregation. The writer to the Hebrews surely had reference to the pastor when he admonished the Christian Hebrews to

> *obey them that have the rule over you and submit yourselves: for they watch for your souls, as they that must give account, that they may do it with joy, and not with grief: for that is unprofitable for you* (Hebrews 13:17).

E. Teachers

And he gave some, . . . teachers.

Teachers, given to the church for the purpose of instructing, complete the divine order for the church's complete ministry. It is interesting to note that pastors and teachers are spoken of by the apostle as a team. It should be noted that apostles, prophets, and evangelists are given to the church individually, each of them in a distinct category and with a particular work to do. Note carefully that it is said that he gave some *pastors and teachers*—combining the two, yet giving each distinct recognition. This indicates that the pastor and teacher, though with different responsibilities, are placed in the church to work as a divine team.

The relationship of the pastor (shepherd) and the teacher (instructor) is a close relationship indeed. It is such a close relationship that their work often overlaps. It indicates that the pastor is to devote time to teaching, while the teacher may be called upon to tend the flock in ways other than teaching. Ideally the pastor is "teaching" as he preaches and the teacher is "preaching" as he teaches. The preaching ministry and the teaching ministry are indeed inseparable. The God-ordained plan, that of the pastor and the teacher as a team in His service, cannot be improved upon by man.

The Lord in His wisdom has seen fit to include in the divine order of the ministry of the church, apostles, or personal representatives; prophets, inspired to foretell and forthtell His truths; evangelists, to herald the Good News to those who have not heard it; pastors, to care for and watch over the flock; and teachers, to instruct in the ways of the Lord and to set the example of believers in observing His commandments. This places the teacher in fellowship with a most distinguished company dedicated and consecrated for the work of the ministry.

A review of the above passage will reveal that it was God who gave some apostles and some prophets and some pastors and teachers

THE TEACHER

to the church. This is evidence that God has provided the church all that is needed for an effective ministry.

Some churches may need an apostle for a particular work, and God gave the apostles to do it. Another church might need a forthteller for an effective ministry, and God gave the prophet to fill that need. Yet another church may have a pressing need for an evangelist, and God made the one who is to herald the Good News available to the church.

The Lord recognized that the need for pastors and teachers would be great in the church, and that need was supplied through the called ministers and consecrated teachers. This is indeed a Scriptural team for the work of the ministry and for the edifying of the body of Christ.

II. The Immediate Goal of the Teacher

The ministry of the teacher has been placed on a plane of equal importance with that of the apostles, the prophets, the evangelists, and the pastor. Each of these workers, in order to be effective, must have a goal or goals. The apostle Paul sets before us the *immediate* goal of the teacher. To be most exact, he sets forth three immediate goals toward which the teacher should strive.

A. The Perfecting of the Saints

Two words demand attention—"perfecting" and "saints." In the sense in which it is used here, the word *perfect* means "sacred, pure, or blameless." The combined efforts of the apostles, the prophets, the evangelists, the pastors, and the teachers is to "completely furnish" the sacred, pure, and blameless people of the Lord. That is the absolutely essential aim of teaching—providing the necessary equipment for living among men and witnessing to them concerning the things of the Lord.

The teacher's responsibility in providing this instruction for Christian living is of great importance. It is the teacher who is primarily responsible for the accomplishment of the third phase of the commission as is given in Matthew 28:20. The church is admonished to be engaged in the work of

> ... *teaching them to observe all things whatsoever I have commanded you. ...*

The saints are not completely furnished if they have only heard the message, *they must be taught!* The teacher, therefore, must become well acquainted with the only textbook the Lord made available for teaching His message—the Bible. Paul reminded Timothy that

> *All scripture is given by inspiration of God, and is profitable for doctrine, for reproof, for correction, for instruction in righteousness: That the man of God may be perfect, thoroughly furnished unto all good works* (II Timothy 3:16-17).

One of the immediate goals of the teacher is to perfect (completely equip) the saints. This can be accomplished only as men make diligent preparation and effective presentation of the Word of the Lord, the inspired message from God to man!

B. The Work of the Ministry

The Christian teacher must bear in mind that his contribution to the cause of Christ is most significant in that his efforts are to further the work of the ministry. The work of the ministry may be considered to be the combined efforts of those who are engaged in serving or attending those reached with the Gospel. The teacher is truly a servant in that he is to attend to the spiritual needs of those whom he teaches. The work of the ministry cannot be considered

THE TEACHER

complete without the dedicated efforts of committed teachers who are engaged in teaching the great truths of the Bible.

It is by and through this dedication of the teachers that others are prepared to teach. The church of Galatia was admonished to

Let him that is taught in the word communicate unto him that teacheth in all good things (Galatians 6:6).

The primary meaning of this passage is that those who are taught by the teacher should share with their teacher the necessary things for living. This is the same principle that was enunciated by Moses when he declared that the ox which treadeth out the corn should not be muzzled.

But there is another great truth to be gleaned from this statement of Galatians 6:6. It should also be considered as an admonition to those who have already learned a particular truth from the Bible to share that truth with others, especially the ones who are bearing the burden of teaching. Paraphrased, we may read it like this, "Let him that has already been taught the Word of the Lord share his knowledge and insight with those who are to teach the Word."

It is through passing gained knowledge to others that the work of the ministry is carried forward from generation to generation.

C. The Edifying of the Body of Christ

The third immediate goal of the teacher is to edify or build up the body of Christ, the church. Actually, we are told, this is not a third goal to be reached but rather a result of the attainment of the first two mentioned goals. It is because of the tremendous importance of all church members, and teachers in particular, striving to build up the church that we include this as a major goal of the Christian teacher. Most definitely every act of the Christian should be with the intention and purpose of building up the work of the Lord on earth.

Webster's New World Dictionary defines the word "edify" as "to instruct or improve morally or spiritually." Surely this must have been in the mind of Paul as he wrote to the Ephesian Christians. He recognized that the efforts of the apostles, prophets, evangelists, pastors, and teachers were necessary to accomplish the goal of instructing and improving the saints in moral and spiritual values.

III. The Ultimate Goals of the Teacher

The long range goal of the Christian teacher is set forth in verse 13:

> *Till we all come in the unity of the faith, and of the Son of God, unto a perfect man, unto the measure of the stature of the fullness of Christ.*

This passage reveals a fourfold ultimate goal of the Christian teacher: 1) That we all should reach unity in the faith, 2) that we all should attain the highest knowledge of the Son of God, 3) that we all should become fully developed Christians, and 4) that each Christian should come to know Christ as He really is.

A. That We All Should Reach Unity in the Faith

The dedicated Christian teacher longs for the day when there will be oneness in the faith. Many differences of opinion divide serious and sincere teachers now, but those who are truly concerned with the teaching of the Word of God look forward to the day when there shall be oneness, agreement, among teachers and other concerned Christians, concerning the Word of the Lord.

Dedicated Christian teachers have a longing for that day when all are persuaded that God's Word is infallible, inspired, eternal, and an all-sufficient rule of faith and practice. A desire to see all peoples give credence to the commands and the prohibitions of the Lord is ever present in the heart of truly concerned Christians. They desire

THE TEACHER

that all should have such deep moral convictions that all would have complete reliance upon Christ as Saviour. All this, and much more, is involved in the unity of the faith.

B. That All Should Attain the Highest Knowledge of Jesus

On one occasion the apostle Paul exclaimed,

That I may know him, and the power of his resurrection, and the fellowship of his sufferings, being made conformable unto his death (Philippians 3:10).

This is the burning desire of every Christian, especially Christian teachers. To know Christ in the power of His resurrection is to have the privilege of walking with Him in newness of life. The death to sin and the resurrection to a new life for the Christian is a transforming experience.

Paul also spoke of knowing the fellowship of the sufferings of his Lord. Although Paul's life had been devoted to teaching others the way of the Lord, he longed for this unusual and blessed fellowship of the Lord's sufferings. It is a responsibility of the teachers of the Word of the Lord to teach the followers of Christ that they, too, are to aspire to this plane of Christian living.

But there is something even greater to be known by the Christian teacher than the power of Christ's resurrection or the fellowship of His sufferings. Paul wanted to *know* Christ. Is this not the earnest desire of every Christian teacher—to know Christ fully and to have the privilege of introducing others to Him? Is not this the grand climax of all the many challenges of the Christian teacher?

C. That We All Should Be Fully Developed Christians

No greater blessing can come to the church than to have those of her membership to be mature, fully developed followers of the Lord

Jesus Christ. On the other hand, what is more distressing than the bickering, backbiting, envious actions of church members who have, for many years, remained only "babes in Christ"? The Christian teacher is often distressed over the lack of spiritual understanding among the people of the Lord and, though it is most often a long process, it is the goal of the Christian teacher to see this sad condition overcome. It can be overcome only as the people of the Lord grow in faith and in the knowledge of the Lord. Stunted Christians all around us are reminders that the long-range goals of the Christian teacher must be kept in sight and among these goals is the growth of men and women in the church into stalwart Christians.

D. That We All Might Know Christ in Person

Knowing Christ fully must be the greatest of all the desires of the Christian teacher. But this experience must await the return of the Lord when He shall come to take away His own from the earth. John declared that,

> ... It doth not yet appear what we shall be: but we know that, when he shall appear, we shall be like him; for we shall see him as he is (I John 3:2).

The Christian teacher is concerned with teaching man the things of the Lord, introducing him to Christ as Saviour, and preparing him to come face to face with Christ. It is then, when man comes face to face with the Lord, that he shall know Christ in fullness.

IV. The Final Results of Teaching

In Ephesians 4:14 Paul declared,

> That we henceforth be no more children, tossed to and fro, and carried about with every wind of doctrine, by

THE TEACHER

the sleight of men, and cunning craftiness, whereby they lie in wait to deceive.

At least three distinct and final results of teaching are set forth in this passage. There are many others of which the Bible speaks, but the three set forth here are of particular interest to the dedicated teacher. They are:

A. Maturity in Christian Grace

That we henceforth be no more children. . . .

Without doubt one of the most challenging opportunities of the Christian teacher is to provide spiritual food for the newborn babe in Christ. As a result of receiving this food, the soul of the newborn Christian matures. The appalling number of undeveloped Christians in the average church is a sad commentary upon the teaching ministry of the church. A twenty-year-old infant is not normal because something in his body has failed to function normally. A person who has been a Christian for twenty years but has not experienced spiritual growth and development and is still a spiritual infant is strong evidence that something in the church has failed to function normally! Most often this failure can be traced to the teaching ministry of that church. As the infant who fails to develop physically cannot be held responsible for this failure to develop, so the young Christian cannot be held responsible for failure to mature in Christian grace if the church cannot or will not provide proper spiritual nourishment.

Paul found it necessary to feed the Corinthian Christians with milk and not with meat because they had failed to develop sufficient spiritual maturity to partake of the meat of the Word. Paul did not refuse to feed these Christians because of their inability to eat what they should have been eating, but rather *he fed them with the food that was necessary for them at that time.* So is it the responsibility of the Christian teacher of today; he must provide the food that his pupils can assimilate. It is a challenging undertaking for the teacher to determine the spiritual needs of those whom he is teaching and to provide the spiritual food necessary to supply those needs fully!

There are two extremes against which the Christian teacher must be constantly on guard. One extreme is that of offering his pupils nothing but "milk"; the other is to offer them nothing but "meat." Both these extremes are dangerous and will lead to stunted spiritual growth if the teacher persists in following either. Yet, both "milk" and "meat" are an absolute necessity if the proper spiritual growth is to be attained. As it is most absurd to offer an infant of six months a rib steak for his lunch each day, so it is absurd to expect a newly-saved person to be able to assimilate the strong meat of the Word as soon as he is saved. On the other hand, what is more out of harmony with the teaching of the Bible and out of touch with reality than expecting adult men who are required to do hard labor to sit down to three meals of "milk" each day? The point is that there are phases of life and circumstances when "milk" is absolutely necessary and other phases when "meat" is demanded. The challenge of the teacher is to recognize the need for each as it arises and to supply it when demanded.

B. Stability

That we henceforth be no more . . . tossed to and fro. . . .

Stability in Christian living is closely related to and dependent upon the degree of spiritual maturity one has attained. In fact, the lack of Christian stability is an indication of Christian immaturity. The Christian of the twentieth century needs, and needs desperately, a stabilizing force in his life. The teacher of the Word of the Lord has a golden opportunity to "root and ground" his pupils in the inspired Word of the Lord. This rooting and grounding in Bible

THE TEACHER

principles and explicit teachings will serve as an anchor of the soul and insure that those who are thus taught may not be tossed to and fro by the forces of evil rampant in the world. There are so many powers of evil preying upon unwary Christians and so many overwhelming temptations to face, it is imperative that the Christian teacher put forth every effort to prepare his pupils for these circumstances. The teacher can rejoice in the knowledge that those whom he has taught can be profoundly affected by the power of this teaching as they seek stability for their lives. The Christian teacher, after he has diligently taught, will then in love commend them to Jesus who can,

> ... *after that ye have suffered a while, make you perfect, stablish, strengthen, settle you.* (II Peter 5:10).

A definite result of effective teaching is mature, stabilized Christians. This, of course, in turn produces strong, Christ-honoring churches.

C. Orthodoxy

> *That we henceforth be no more ... carried about with every wind of doctrine.*

The church member who knows what the Bible teaches, believes it, and acts upon it is indeed a blessing to his church. An even greater blessing to the church is that teacher who is endued with the ability to teach others what the message of the Bible is and to persuade them to accept this as a rule of faith and practice. It has often been said concerning some individual that, "He knows what he believes and why he believes it." This may or may not be a compliment to that individual! More necessary than mere belief is a sound basis for it. The basis of the Christian's beliefs must be the Bible. It must be the one rule of his faith and practice. The Christian teacher has a tremendous influence in producing orthodoxy in the church of the Lord Jesus Christ.

There are many "winds" of doctrine blowing upon man today. Some of these doctrines are true to the teachings of the Bible while others are far from it. The end result of effective teaching is that even though the winds of false doctrines blow upon man, he will not be "carried about" by them. Some of these "winds" of doctrine come as gentle breezes while others are apt to come upon one as a tornado. Either the breezes or the tornadoes of false doctrines can do great harm to one's spiritual life if they are permitted to carry him about at will. Most individuals find the gentle breezes of false doctrine often more difficult to cope with than the tornadoes of these doctrines. So often the gentle breezes are so imperceptible that one is carried far away from the harbor of orthodoxy before he realizes what is happening to him.

Christian teachers must come to the realization that they are powerless to prevent the various "winds of doctrine" from blowing upon those whom they teach. With this realization, it is imperative that the teacher resolve to so teach that his pupils will be saturated with the doctrines of Christ to the extent that they will not be "carried about" with false teachings. The only sure antidote to false doctrine is the truth as it is given in the Bible, the textbook of the effective teacher.

V. The Manner of Teaching

But speaking the truth in love, may grow up into him in all things, which is the head, even Christ.

"Speaking the truth in love"—this is a most significant phrase when considered as an admonition to the Christian teacher. Note these words of special import—"speaking," "truth," and "love." They indicate a threefold responsibility of the teacher.

THE TEACHER

A. Speak

It is the responsibility of the teacher to speak out as he faces his class. He has something to say which is most important and as yet is unknown to many of those in his class. For this very reason the teacher must be prepared to "speak out" on the truths of the Bible. Successful teaching demands that those who teach accept the responsibility of *leading* in the discussion of each lesson. The teacher is not a "follower" of his class but rather is a "leader" in every sense of the word. Consequently he must be prepared not only to *lead out* in the lesson but to *guide* the discussion by the various members of the class unit.

B. Speak the Truth

It is not sufficient that the teacher merely speak; it is the content of what he says that is so important. The teacher is divinely obligated to impart the truth in his teaching; anything less than the truth is foreign to the will and purpose of the Lord. Because of the tremendous challenge to speak the truth, the teacher will surely recognize the importance of research and study as well as fervent prayer before presenting material as truth.

Jesus said,

Ye shall know the truth and the truth shall make you free (John 8:32).

Indeed, the teacher must recognize his most important role in God's plan for the freeing of man from sin. The Christian teacher is often the key to freedom for the searching soul. Since the teacher is to speak the truth and the truth is used of the Lord to bring freedom to men, the teacher will do well to remember his responsibility in conveying this truth to those who will receive it.

C. Speak the Truth in Love

The Christian teacher is admonished to speak the truth in *love.* Love must be the highest motivation for Christian teaching: love for Christ, love for souls, love for the truth, love for the church, and love for the teaching ministry.

1. The love for Jesus

The Christian teacher is obligated to declare the truth because the love of Jesus constrains him to do so. Jesus will never be pleased with anything less than the truth, the whole truth and nothing but the truth! To a large degree, the love the teacher has for Jesus will determine the kind of teacher he will be. The teacher will not only *talk* of his love for the Lord; his life will be living proof that it is genuine!

2. Love for Souls

Teachers must speak the truth in love to the souls of those whom they teach. Nothing is more precious than the immortal souls of men. Because the effective teacher is always mindful of the fact that souls are at stake, he speaks truthfully, though it may sometimes offend and occasionally alienate the person to whom he is speaking. The truly effective teacher is not so much concerned with his personal relationship with the pupil as he is with the relationship between the pupil and the Lord Jesus Christ.

3. Love for the Truth

Successful teaching demands that the teacher have a love for the truth itself.

THE TEACHER

> *Study to shew thyself approved unto God, a workman that needeth not to be ashamed, rightly dividing the Word of truth* (II Timothy 2:15).

This word of admonition from Paul to Timothy is certainly applicable to the Christian teacher. Love for the truth itself will constrain the teacher to diligently seek it. Paul declared in the above passage that God's approval upon one's life is dependent upon one's study. Christian teachers study to ascertain the truth for themselves and then pass this knowledge along to those whom they teach.

Another reason for loving the truth is revealed in the statement,

> *A workman that needeth not to be ashamed. . . .*

Sooner or later, the teacher who fails to seek out the truth will find himself ashamed before men and before God. Teachers need never fear being ashamed so long as they continue to seek out the truth, love it, and declare it to others while being a living example of the power of the truth.

> *May grow up into him in all things. . . .*

This is teaching by example! Surely the teacher must be an example of what he teaches. It is worthy of note that the Lord has made frequent use of the terms "grow up," "perfect," "mature," with reference to those who would teach. The world is looking for an example to follow and the Christian teacher should be anxious to provide that example. The teacher will note too that the Lord Himself is the Example to follow.

> *Which is the head, even Christ.*

Effective teachers follow the directions of the Lord and set the example for others to do likewise.

For further discussion on the importance of love in the teaching ministry, the reader is referred to Chapter 3, "Motivation," which deals with this subject in depth.

2
THE CHALLENGE

THE EFFECTIVE TEACHER
PLAYS A MOST VITAL ROLE
IN MOLDING CHARACTER
FOR TIME AND ETERNITY.

2
THE CHALLENGE

A tremendous responsibility rests upon those who have been selected by the church to teach the Word of the Lord in this age of skepticism, secularism, and modernism. Teaching is a most holy and high calling and should be entered into only after prayerful and honest self-examination. The responsibility of the Christian teacher is pointed out clearly in II Timothy 2:2:

And the things which thou hast heard of me among many witnesses, the same commit thou to faithful men, who shall be able to teach others also.

The phrase, "... commit thou to faithful men...," indicates that the teacher is to share his knowledge of the Bible with others, who in turn shall be enabled to share their knowledge with others following them. Thus the Word of the Lord is to be taught diligently from one generation to the next. It is the challenge of the teacher to maintain the purity of the Word in all his teaching.

I. The Challenge of the Teacher

The real challenge of the teacher is to be considered in the following areas: 1) He is to retain the purity of the Word in all his teaching. 2) He is to excel as a leader among men. 3) He is to prepare others for the great responsibility of teaching. 4) He is to have an appreciation of his importance as a teacher. 5) He is to use wisely the time allotted him for his teaching.

A. Retain the Purity of the Word

The purity of the Word must be retained if Christ's body, His church, is to prosper, but this will not be accomplished through the efforts of the ordained minister alone. Remember that the teacher and the pastor are set in the church as a team for the edifying of the body of Christ. While the pastor may make every effort to preach the Word and remain true to the Bible, unless those who occupy the classrooms also accept this great responsibility, many will be led astray.

In some respects, the influence of the teacher is greater than that of the minister. This is especially true with reference to those in the younger age brackets. The same is true concerning many adults, for, though it is a sad state of affairs, there are many who attend Sunday school who seldom or never hear the minister preach. The Christian teacher is faced with a most significant challenge to make certain that God's Word is taught in its purity in the classroom.

B. Excel as a Leader among Men

The teacher must also accept the burden of responsibility resting upon him as a leader. To effectively discharge this responsibility, the teacher must set a Christian example. He must recognize that he is under close surveillance and that what he *does* is often more profound and far reaching than what he *says*. This is especially true if his conduct is not in harmony with the teaching of the Bible. The teacher whose conduct is at variance with his teaching will have an influence upon his class, but it will be a bad influence rather than a good one.

THE CHALLENGE

The admonition of Paul to the church in Corinth is particularly applicable to the teacher:

What? Know ye not that your body is the temple of the Holy Ghost which is in you, which you have of God, and you are not your own? For you are bought with a price: therefore glorify God in your body, and in your spirit, which are God's (I Corinthians 6:19-20).

The dedicated teacher will recognize the intrinsic value of keeping himself "unspotted from the world" in order that he may exert the right influence upon those whom he teaches.

In a very real sense the teacher is truly not his own. In the first place he belongs to God—soul and body. It is especially tragic for those charged with the responsibility of teaching others the Word of God to assume that God has a claim only on his soul. While it is certainly a fact that Jesus purchased the soul, it must be remembered that He also purchased the body. As a possession of the Lord under the management of man, the body, as well as the soul, must be dedicated to the Lord. This is what Paul meant:

I beseech you therefore, brethren, by the mercies of God, that you present your bodies a living sacrifice, holy, acceptable unto God, which is your reasonable service (Romans 12:1).

The key to effective teaching is found in this statement: "Present your *bodies* a *living sacrifice,* holy, acceptable unto God." This is possible only as the teacher accepts the full burden of responsibility resting upon him as a teacher. The body must become a *living sacrifice* for God. The inordinate desires of the flesh must be sacrificed if the teacher is to be effective in his work.

Yielding to the "aches and pains" to which all our physical bodies are subject is a luxury the effective teacher will deny himself. While many church members, some of them his pupils, will be kept at home by some insignificant or imagined ailment, the truly effective teacher will ignore ailments which are far more bothersome.

To attain success as a teacher there must be a sacrifice of time. While other church members are devoting much of their time to the unnecessary and often spiritually harmful activities of the world, the concerned teacher is spending much time in preparation for teaching. Studying the Bible, the quarterly, commentaries, a Bible atlas, and other related material is time consuming, but the effective teacher has learned to sacrifice his personal desires to provide sufficient time for adequate preparation. He also has spent much time in becoming acquainted with the needs of his pupils by studying them in their homes, at church, at play, and other places.

The burden of leadership is a tremendous challenge for the teacher. He will lead by word and deed. He will lead in church activities designed to develop other Christian leaders. His leadership in helping to make the total church program evangelistic, didactic, missionary, and devotional is essential if he is to reach his full potential. He will set the example in faithfulness in all church activities. The effective teacher is convinced that the church is the one qualified organization to promulgate the Gospel of Christ; and he will devote his energy, his talents, his knowledge, and his influence to this end.

C. Prepare Others for the Responsibility of Teaching

Effective teachers must recognize the responsibility they have assumed as they prepare others to take their places. Much concern has been expressed about the church of tomorrow. The question is being asked as to what kind of church it will be. The answer is simple; the church of tomorrow will be the kind of church we make it today! To a great extent this is determined by the type of teaching being done in the church now. The teacher truly concerned about

THE CHALLENGE

the future of the church has recognized that he is preparing someone to fill the place of responsibility now occupied by himself. One day the teacher will teach his last lesson; the preacher will preach his last message; the singer will sing his last song; the soul winner will win his last soul; and the responsibility for these activities will pass into the hands of those whom today's leaders have prepared. *The great challenge is to properly prepare for these responsibilities before they are assumed.* The effective teacher recognizes this sobering fact and makes diligent efforts to assure continued Bible-oriented and Christ-centered teaching in the church after his departure.

D. Appreciate Your Importance

The effective teacher has an appreciation of his importance. While he recognizes his unworthiness without the sustaining and spiritually strengthening grace of God, he will recognize his importance not because of *who* he is but because of *what* he is. There are many reasons why he is important. One of the most sobering aspects of this importance is that he is dealing with the most precious possession of those whom he teaches—immortal souls. Without doubt the Christian teacher is included in the statement of James:

Brethren, if any of you do err from the truth, and one convert him; Let him know, that he which converteth the sinner from the error of his way shall save a soul from death, and shall hide a multitude of sins (James 5:19-20).

It is most important for the Christian teacher to recognize that God has ordained that teaching is effective in converting (turning about) erring saints as well as bringing the message of salvation to the lost. The teacher is concerned with eternal values. The soul of man is at stake and the effective teacher bears this in mind at all times. Statistics reveal that the vast majority of those who are saved have come under the influence of a Christian teacher—usually in the Sunday school. Viewed in the light of these proven statistics, the influence of the teacher cannot be minimized. He is important to the seeking child, the confused teen-ager, the groping adult, and all of those who have somehow lost their way in this maze of sin. The effective teacher will realize that these disturbed individuals are seeking help from God and that he is God's representative in the classroom.

The effective teacher realizes that his place of service affords him an excellent opportunity to teach his pupils life's important principles. Those Christian workers who have high ideals and have built their lives upon principles that endure are those who have been taught the Word of God. A profane person is never a truly great person. The Word of God coupled with the power of the Holy Spirit will mold and fashion character which is God honoring. The teacher has the privilege and responsibility of teaching that Word! The effective teacher plays a vital role in molding character for time and eternity. It has been said that the Christian experience only prepares one to die. While this experience does prepare one to die, it also is the one experience that prepares one to live! The non-Christian is neither prepared to *live* nor to *die*. Consideration of this sobering fact causes the Christian teacher to realize more fully his importance.

Teachers of the Word of the Lord represent the greatest cause on earth—the cause of Christ. As the teacher teaches he does so with the assurance and awesome realization that he is indeed God's representative. This is no work of small importance! The Word of God is quick, and powerful, and sharper than any two-edged sword. The teacher must wield it in the classroom and in his personal life with the realization that it is having a profound effect on men. This is a tremendous responsibility.

THE CHALLENGE

E. Wisely Use Your Time

The realization that effective teaching produces and promotes fellowship among Christians will remind the teacher of the importance of the right use of his time both in and out of the classroom. The teacher must remember that at the most he has only thirty or thirty-five minutes of time to devote to teaching during the class period. The brevity of this time will dictate that the time be used for *teaching*.

While socials are good and can fill a definite need in modern-day churches, the teacher must insist that plans and preparations for socials be made at some time other than that set aside for teaching. A called meeting some night during the week or an early meeting on Sunday morning should be utilized for the purpose of planning socials.

The time set aside for teaching should not be spent in discussing current events, sports, or politics except as they may relate directly to the lesson. Although Christians should have an active interest in community affairs, the discussion of these should be some time other than that intended for the class period.

The public schools demand that our children attend classes thirty-five or more *hours* per week in order that they may be given a well-rounded education. It requires this much time for the public schools to teach the pupil how to make a living, while the Christian teacher is given only thirty or thirty-five *minutes* per week to teach him how to live! When viewed in this perspective it is apparent that the teacher's brief time for teaching is too precious to allow it to be misused.

The successful teacher is submissive to the will of the church. The fact that the church sets one apart to teach is within itself an important consideration. There are without doubt many in the church who are qualified to teach but are not chosen to do so. Under the leadership of the Holy Spirit the church chooses one rather than another. This should challenge the chosen to give their best in this ministry. There is no higher authority for teaching the Word of the Lord than the Church of the Lord Jesus Christ. The teacher must recognize this authority and submit himself to the will of the church in all things.

II. The Rewards of Christian Teaching

The rewards for Christian teachers are many although they are often intangible. Some of the rich rewards reserved for dedicated teachers are: 1) the salvation of souls, 2) informed church members, 3) responsible church leaders, and 4) fellowship in the church.

A. The Salvation of Souls

The salvation of souls as a result of teaching efforts is surely the greatest reward. Many teachers shall have a reward from the Lord for winning some souls to Christ even though the teacher is not aware of winning these particular people to the Lord. We often read or hear of a great ingathering of souls during a revival, and the community involved probably attributes the success of the effort to the visiting evangelist or the pastor. People talk of the great evangelist who preached the revival. While this is not intended to minimize the work of the evangelist, it must nevertheless be recognized that some or all of the souls saved in the revival were the result of the dedicated efforts of consecrated teachers. Sunday after Sunday and week after week, though often discouraged, consecrated teachers kept at their post of duty and expounded the Word of the Lord to what appeared to be deaf ears! Yet when the revival came the fruit of the labor of these teachers was revealed in the salvation of those taught. This should encourage the teacher.

B. Informed Church Members

Another reward for effective teaching is a church with *informed* members. Perhaps one of the great tragedies of our time is the appalling number of churches whose vast majority of members have no real knowledge of what the Bible teaches. While it is true to some extent that all churches have uninformed members, successful teachers will be actively concerned with informing the uninformed members as well as winning the lost. To see a church member grow in grace and knowledge is a real reward for the truly concerned teacher. Defenders of the faith are needed in all churches, and the teacher who knows he has had a part in developing defenders of the faith is indeed a blessed man.

C. Responsible Church Leaders

It is rewarding to the teacher to see those whom he has taught accept places of responsibility assigned to them by the church. As has already been noted, the day will come when someone must take the place of the most effective and dedicated teacher in the church. To relinquish this responsibility to those whom one has taught should be a most satisfying experience.

D. Fellowship in the Church

Successful teaching produces fellowship among church members. The divisions, bickerings, backbiting, and envy that characterize many churches will be eliminated when souls are saved and taught how to live as Christians.

There are definite requirements to be met if real fellowship is to prevail in the church. These requirements are set forth in the Bible, and the teacher of the Bible must accept the challenge of teaching these to his pupils. Real teaching is effectual only if that which is taught is translated into action.

II. Difficulties Encountered

The long-range goals and the immediate goals of the teacher discussed in the preceding chapter are the ideal for which every dedicated teacher will strive. However, the many obstacles and hindrances encountered in the quest of these goals make them most difficult to attain.

A. Teacher Attitude

Many reasons could be cited for the difficulties encountered in reaching the desired goals of the teacher but they are most succinctly stated by Paul in his admonition to Timothy:

> *.. be instant in season, out of season; reprove, rebuke, exhort with all longsuffering and doctrine. For the time will come when they will not endure sound doctrine; but after their own lusts shall they heap to themselves teachers, having itching ears; and they shall turn away their ears from the truth, and shall be turned unto fables* (II Timothy 4:2-4).

The Phillips translation makes the meaning somewhat more meaningful to the teacher:

> *... Never lose your sense of urgency, in season or out of season. Prove, correct, and encourage, using the utmost patience in your teaching. For the time is coming when men will not tolerate wholesome teaching. They will want something to tickle their own fancies, and they will collect teachers who will pander to their own desires. They will no longer listen to the truth, but will wander off after man-made fictions.*

THE CHALLENGE

While it is recognized that Paul's admonition was addressed to a young minister, it is evident that the charge is applicable to the teacher as well. A teaching situation demands that we have a teacher, a pupil, and a lesson. Each of these is mentioned by Paul in this passage.

Note that the teacher is admonished to:

1. Never lose his sense of urgency.
2. Prove or establish the validity or authenticity of his message.
3. Correct or make right the wrongs in the life of the pupil.
4. Encourage or give hope and confidence to those whom he teaches.
5. Have patience in the process of applying the above principles of effective teaching.

B. Pupil Attitude

The pupils of the last days are aptly described by the apostle Paul. They are declared to be such as those who:

1. Will not tolerate or put up with wholesome doctrine (or teaching).
2. Will desire to hear only those things which will tickle their ears or will not alarm them.
3. Will seek teachers who will pander to their lustful desires.
4. Will not give attention to the truth.
5. Will follow man-made tales or doctrines.

C. Church Attitude

Though the attitude of the teacher and that of the pupil has much to do with the success or lack of success in the teaching ministry, there is another important consideration for attaining effective teaching. The attitude of the church is most important. It must be such that the teacher will be both encouraged and inspired as well as equipped with all necessary materials for teaching.

It is not enough that the church merely select some of its members to serve as teachers. It is imperative that the church supply all the necessary tools for teaching. There must be a manifest and continued interest in the teachers as individuals. If the attitude of the church is such that teachers cannot have complete assurance of the backing of the church, they are most apt to fall short of the desired teaching goals.

To sum up the difficulties encountered in reaching the goal of effective teaching, the teacher, the pupil, and the church must work together in harmony with the same goals in mind.

The lesson taught by the teacher is to be:

1. Doctrinal, though some will not endure it.

2. Wholesome, tending to improve the mind or morals.

3. Truth, based upon fact, not fancy.

The effective teacher recognizes the urgency of his mission and makes every effort to meet the challenge presented him. He establishes the authenticity of his teaching by basing it entirely upon the Bible. He strives to assist the pupil to correct the errors of his life through an experience of salvation through Jesus Christ and a life committed to Him. The effective teacher encourages those whom he teaches, for he recognizes that they, too, have many temptations to overcome. In the process of his teaching, he prays for patience in dealing with those who may be wayward.

Though a teacher is aware of the fact that many will not endure (put up with) his teaching, he must be prepared to endure or put up with the hardships he encounters through the opposition of those who will not hear him. While the teacher is warned that an unbelieving world will not "put up" with him, he must nonetheless be prepared to "put up" with the very people who scorn him. This is the challenge that Paul gave Timothy and it is surely the great challenge of the Christian teacher in these perilous times.

3
MOTIVATION

SUCCESSFUL TEACHERS
HAVE A HIGHER MOTIVATION
THAN THAT PRODUCED
BY THE MERE FACT THAT
SOME CHURCH HAS SELECTED
THEM TO TEACH.

3
MOTIVATION

A *motive* is an inner drive or impulse that causes a person to do something, or to act in a certain way. Everyone experiences some degree of motivation and this is especially true of the Christian teacher.

It is not difficult to determine the motives of some of the more prominent characters of the Bible. A careful study of some Bible characters will reveal the tremendous power of motivation.

Revelation 12:12 reveals the motivation of Satan who is revealed as being cast down to the earth.

> *Therefore rejoice, ye heavens, and ye that dwell in them. Woe to the inhabiters of the earth and of the sea! for the devil is come down unto you, having great wrath, because he knoweth that he hath but a short time.*

It will immediately be noted that Satan was most highly motivated by the knowledge that he had but a brief time in which he was to accomplish his deeds. This disturbing knowledge caused his anger to be so great that a woe was pronounced upon the earth and its inhabitants. This is a most graphic picture of what sufficient motivation will encourage one to do. Note that the Bible says that Satan *knoweth* that his time is short. It would be a real blessing to the church of the twentieth century if all Christian teachers and other concerned workers in God's kingdom would also come to the realization that the time allotted to them is indeed a brief time also. The knowledge of the brevity of time indeed should motivate teachers.

David was motivated by lust when he committed his notorious sins. Having looked upon Bathsheba and lusting after her, he was moved to take whatever action necessary to gratify his lustful desire. This lust led to ever-increasing involvement until eventually a tragedy intervened. The sordid record of events concerning David and Bathsheba is but another commentary upon the power of motivation as it drives one to a course of action, whether that action is good or bad.

Paul was highly motivated as is evident by his exclamation recorded in Romans 9:1-4:

> *I say the truth in Christ, I lie not, my conscience also bearing me witness in the Holy Ghost, That I have great heaviness and continual sorrow in my heart. For I could wish that myself were accursed from Christ for my brethren, my kinsmen according to the flesh: Who are Israelites; to whom pertaineth the adoption, and the glory, and the covenants, and the giving of the law, and the service of God, and the promises. . . .*

The consuming desire of Paul was that his brethren in the flesh might be saved. His urgent goal of witnessing the salvation of souls as a result of his preaching and teaching determined his course of action. So great was his desire to witness the salvation of his kinsmen that he reached the point of being willing to be himself cut off from Christ if it would bring about the salvation of his people. This is indeed motivation in the highest sense of the word.

The list of Bible characters who were highly motivated is inexhaustible.

MOTIVATION

Simon the sorceror was motivated to ask for the power exemplified by the apostles of the Lord Jesus because he had a desire for spiritual power which he was not equipped to receive. Surely this should speak volumes to teachers, preachers, and other Christian workers. God endued us with the power He wishes us to have and which could be utilized by us. Often we hear of a person saying that he would be willing to teach if he could teach like Brother Jones or Smith. Another person may wish to attain the exact and same success of one of his cohorts. Preachers, too, sometimes find themselves saying that they would not mind preaching if they could proclaim the Word with the power of some other brother they have heard preach. This is not the kind of motivation the Lord would have teachers possess. Christian teachers as well as preachers are to dedicate to the Lord the powers and abilities they possess.

Judas was motivated to deny the Lord by a desire for a paltry thirty pieces of silver.

Diotrophes was motivated to cast Christians out of the church because of his insatiable desire for preeminence among the brethren.

Demas was motivated to forsake Paul because of his love for the allurements of this world.

Esther was motivated to risk her life because of her intense desire to see her people freed from bondage.

Gideon was motivated to face a most formidable army of the enemy with his three hundred men because he had faith in God.

Isaiah, following his vision and cleansing, was motivated to proclaim the message of the Lord.

Jesus Christ was motivated to come to this world of sin and sorrow and die for sinners because He loved them with great compassion.

It is evident in both the Old Testament and the New Testament that men who are motivated are apt to be the most persistent in their efforts to attain the goals that they have set for themselves or that others have set for them. This is true whether the motivation is for a good cause or for a bad one.

Effective teachers of this age are motivated too. They have an inner drive that compels them to make the sacrifices necessary to accomplish their goals. Effective teachers have a higher motivation than that produced by the mere fact that they have been selected by a church to teach. Though their selection by the church is surely to some degree a motivating factor, there are many other conditions and circumstances that move effective teachers to teach with assurance and satisfaction. Of these, we shall note a few here.

I. Motivated by Love

Webster's New World Dictionary defines *love* as "a strong affection for, or attachment to, or devotion to a person or persons." The Christian teacher certainly must have a strong affection for and attachment to those things that are spiritual. What are some of the objects of the real teacher's love?

A. Love for Christ

Effective and successful teachers love the Lord. Paul wrote to the Christians at Corinth,

> *For whether we be beside ourselves, it is to God: or whether we be sober, it is for your cause. For the love of Christ constraineth us. . . ."* (II Corinthians 5:13-14).

This same passage in other versions will give some added meaning to the thought expressed by Paul if the student will consider them diligently.

MOTIVATION

Phillips:

If we are 'mad' it is for God's glory; if we are perfectly sane it is for your benefit. At any rate there has been no selfish motive. The very spring of our actions is the love of Christ.

The New English Bible:

It may be we are beside ourselves, but it is for God; If we are in our right mind, it is for you. For the love of Christ leaves us no choice. . . .

The Revised Standard Version:

For if we are beside ourselves, it is for God; if we are in our right mind, it is for you. For the love of Christ controls us. . . .

James Moffett Version:

I am beside myself, am I? Well that is between myself and God. I am sane, am I? Well, that is in your interests; for I am controlled by the love of Christ.

The Amplified Bible:

For if we are beside ourselves (mad, as some say), it is for God and concerns Him; If we are in our right mind, it is for your benefit, For the love of Christ controls and urges and impels us. . . .

Careful study of these six versions will reveal more fully the motivating force of the love of Christ.

Christ's love "constrains" according to the King James Version of the Bible. The primary meaning of that word *constrain* is "to bind or draw together—to draw tight."

Those who are engaged in the challenging work of teaching others the way of the Lord can appreciate more fully the meaning of this term because they have learned by experience and observation that the love of Christ is the force that binds them together. It is the drawing power of this love that brings them together in earnest prayer for divine guidance, for clarity of thought, for clearness of presentation, and for the spiritual welfare of those whom they teach. It is this wonderful love that holds them together and binds them in one purpose consistently week after week and month after month and year after year.

The Phillips Version declares that the love of Christ is the "spring of our actions." This indicates that this love is the source, the origin, and the motive of action. Any work done in the name of the Lord which is not done in love for the Lord is vain! This love must always be the source of action on the part of the Christian teacher. *Teaching prompted by love, preceded by prayer, predicated on the Bible, and presented with enthusiasm* will produce desirable results in the classroom and in the lives of those taught.

The New English Version declares that the love of Christ "*leaves us no choice.*" How true this is concerning the teaching of the Word of the Lord. The Christian teacher has no choice other than to remain absolutely true to the Word of God in his teaching. The love of Christ shed abroad in the heart of the teacher leaves him no alternative other than his submission to the will of the Lord in all things. The Christian teacher must at all times be motivated by the love of the Lord or he will never succeed as a teacher.

The Revised Standard Version reminds us that the "*love of Christ controls*" us. Thus we conclude that the love Christ has for us and the love we have for Him exercises a restraining power over the teacher and causes him to submit to the authority of the Lord and to become subject to His commands. The effective teacher prays

MOTIVATION

that the directive will of the Lord may be known to him and that he may obtain the grace needed to be completly submissive to that perfect will of the Lord.

The Amplified Bible says that *"the love of Christ controls, urges, and impels us."* To urge is to exert a force upon one that drives that person to action. The Christian teacher, because of his abiding love for Christ and the great love Christ has for him, is often driven to a course of action that is personally distasteful to him. He recognizes, however, that if he is to remain true to his calling he must initiate the action urged upon him by the leadership of the Holy Spirit.

To impel is to push, drive, or move forward. The effective teacher is concerned with going forward for (and *with*) the Lord Jesus Christ. Successful teaching demands that there be no regression. This explains why the teachers and other leaders of the church are constantly urging the church forward in dedication, consecration, attendance, and in spiritual knowledge and development. The love of Christ truly constrains the Christian teacher to go forward and to urge others to accompany him on his course of action.

The Christian teacher, then, is motivated highly by the unfathomable love of Christ. In this love he is:

1. Drawn together with others who share his responsibilities and privileges.

2. Assured of the source of his impulses.

3. Left no choice other than to submit to the divine will of the Lord.

4. Controlled in all his actions.

5. Urged and compelled to ever greater efforts to reach the goal of effective Christian work.

No greater blessing can come to the Christian teacher or to his pupils than motivation by the unfathomable love of the Lord Jesus Christ.

B. Love for the Truth

All scripture is given by inspiration of God, and is profitable for doctrine, for reproof, for correction, for instruction in righteousness: That the man of God may be perfect, thoroughly furnished unto all good works (II Timothy 3:16).

Because of their conviction that the only textbook that is available to them for inerrant teaching is the Bible, Christian teachers love the Bible for what it is, the Word of the Lord. Teachers who succeed in teaching the Bible believe wholeheartedly in the inspiration of the Scriptures. They accept the Scriptures as a direct communication from God to man. They earnestly subscribe to the doctrine that only the Scriptures, directed by the power of the Holy Spirit, can reprove, rebuke, and exhort sinners. They accept it as the most profitable for doctrine, and because of their profound belief in the Bible being what it claims for itself, they love it fervently.

C. Love for the Church

Christian teachers love the church. Recognizing that Jesus loved the church and gave Himself for her, the teachers who are genuinely concerned with the promulgation of the Gospel have a deep and abiding love for this body of Christ. Paul wrote these words to Timothy nearly two thousand years ago:

These things write I unto thee, hoping to come unto thee shortly: But if I tarry long, that thou mayest know

MOTIVATION

> *how thou oughtest to behave thyself in the house of God, which is the church of the living God, the pillar and ground of the truth* (I Timothy 3:14-15).

Was this not Paul, the teacher, teaching Timothy, the student, how to "busy himself" in the church? Why was he so concerned with Timothy's behavior in the house of God? For the same reason teachers are concerned with behavior in the church today. It was important that Paul teach Timothy the secret of behavior in the early church; how much more important is it in this age for those who are charged with the responsibility of teaching to inform church members how to act in accordance with the will of God! But of more importance is the Christian teacher's privilege of molding character that reveals itself in conduct. The Phillips Translation declares:

> *At the moment of writing I hope to be with you soon, but if there should be any considerable delay then what I have written will show you the sort of character men of God's household ought to have.*

Paul loved the church and recognized its importance in the spread of the Gospel. The teaching ministry today must be concerned with the spread of the Gospel by the church. Effective teaching dictates that the teacher love the church. The depth of the love of the Christian teacher for his church is often revealed in the character and conduct of those whom he has taught.

Love for the church will inspire the teacher to live a dedicated life before those whom he teaches. Recognizing that his life is closely observed, the true teacher will make every effort to maintain purity of thought and deed. This attitude is prompted by the deep love the teacher has for his church and his Lord.

Love for the church will compel the teacher to be faithful in the activities of the church. He will be motivated by this love to cooperate in the total church program. He will show concern for all phases of the church's ministry rather than just the class or department in which he works.

The teacher's love for the church will urge him to set an example for his pupils in church attendance. He will attend all worship services himself and will urge upon his pupils the importance of their doing so. There is no place in the teaching ministry of the church for the teacher who would teach his class and return home before the worship service. The teacher who consistently practices this does not truly love the church. This practice, whether intentional or unintentional, will declare plainly that the teacher does not consider the message of the pastor to be of sufficient importance to warrant his attendance. Successful teachers are motivated by the love they have for the entire ministry of the church—and this emphatically includes the preaching ministry.

D. Love for Souls

An earnest desire to witness the salvation of souls is a characteristic of the effective teacher. While the salvation of souls is not the only purpose of teaching, it is surely one of the most important reasons for Christian teaching. Successful teachers realize the value of an eternal soul. They share the deep feeling of Paul who exclaimed:

> *Brethren, my heart's desire and prayer to God for Israel is, that they might be saved. For I bear them record that they have a zeal of God, but not according to knowledge* (Romans 10:1-2).

This statement reveals the heart of Paul. He desired with all his heart that Israel would be saved. Notice, however, that he implies the necessity of Christian teaching before this could be accom-

MOTIVATION

plished. The phrase "not according to knowledge," indicates that before Israel could undergo the desired experience they must acquire knowledge. Here again is graphically pointed out the great responsibility of those who teach. The lack of knowledge on the part of Israel was a result of a lack of *teaching* on the part of the teachers of that age. Jesus as Saviour had not been presented to them, consequently the Israelites grew from infancy to adulthood without a true knowledge of God! Teachers are placed in the church to assist those who are seeking to attain true knowledge of Jesus as Saviour.

A careful study of the experience of the Philippian jailer reveals that this jailer was not saved simply because Paul and Silas told him to

> *... believe on the Lord Jesus Christ, and thou shalt be saved, and thy house* (Acts 16:31).

Verse 32 declares that Paul and Silas

> *... spake unto him the word of the Lord, and to all that were in his house.*

While we do not have the record of just what was taught this fearful man and his household, we do know that they did teach him about Jesus. This points out the fact that it is not enough for the Christian teacher to tell men to believe on the Lord Jesus Christ for salvation; they must be taught about Jesus and His sacrificial death for sinners.

Teaching *preceded* the *experience* of salvation. Paul and Silas taught the jailer and his household because of the genuine love they possessed for the souls of men.

The Scriptures describe Apollos as

> *... an eloquent man, and mighty in the scriptures. . . . instructed in the way of the Lord; . . . fervent in the*

spirit, he spake and taught diligently the things of the Lord (Acts 18:24-25).

In spite of the splendid attributes of Apollos, he needed instruction concerning some of the things of the Lord, and because Aquila and Priscilla loved him, and the truth, they

... took him unto them, and expounded [taught] unto him the way of God more perfectly (verse 26).

Love for lost souls will motivate Christian teachers to teach them about Jesus and His redeeming grace. Love for those who are saved will motivate true teachers to explain more fully or perfectly the way of God. This is the challenge of the Christian teacher. His personal love for the lost and the saved is a motivating force in his life.

Consider what Paul said:

Though I speak with tongues of men and of angels, and have not charity [love], I am become as sounding brass, or a tinkling cymbal. And though I have the gift of prophecy, and understand all mysteries, and all knowledge; and though I have all faith, so that I could remove mountains, and have not charity [love], I am nothing. And though I bestow all my goods to feed the poor, and though I give my body to be burned, and have not charity [love], it profiteth me nothing (I Corinthians 13:1-3).

Without the motivating force of love the teacher's words are simply and only a noise. They are sounding brass or a tinkling cymbal. Unless love is the spring of all his motives, the undergirding of his knowledge, and the basis of all his faith, the teacher is nothing—of no value or importance. Almsgiving to relieve the hungry or the poor, or martyrdom for the cause of Christ will profit the teacher nothing unless these sacrifices are made as a result of genuine love for God and men.

II. Motivated by World Conditions.

This know also, that in the last days perilous times shall come. For men shall be lovers of their own selves, covetous, boasters, proud, blasphemers, disobedient to parents, unthankful, unholy, Without natural affection, truce-breakers, false accusers, incontinent, fierce, despisers of those that are good, Traitors, heady, highminded, lovers of pleasures more than lovers of God; Having a form of godliness, but denying the power thereof... (II Timothy 3:1-5).

Over nineteen hundred years ago Paul reminded Timothy of the moral, social, and spiritual declension that would characterize the people of the last days. A newspaper editor of today could not more accurately describe conditions of this century than Paul did in his letter to Timothy. The perils of the last days are not floods, storms, hurricanes, tornadoes, earthquakes, or fires. The twentieth-century peril is the attitude of man. The Christian teacher is burdened because of the multitudes who reject the mercies of God offered through Jesus Christ. A careful analysis of Paul's description of man in the last days will reveal twenty descriptive terms used to paint a verbal picture of man as he rushes headlong into judgment.

Man in these last days is:

1. A lover of himself—selfish.
2. Covetous—a lover of money.
3. Boastful—talking of his deeds or abilities.
4. Proud—haughty and arrogant.

5. Blasphemous—lack of reverence for God.

6. Disobedient to parents—unruly.

7. Unthankful—without appreciation.

8. Unholy—completely polluted by sin.

9. Without natural affection—no genuine love.

10. Truce-breakers—undependable.

11. False accusers.

12. Incontinent—without restraint (morally).

13. Fierce—violently cruel.

14. Despisers of those that are good.

15. Traitors—betrayers.

16. Heady—rash, reckless, willful.

17. Highminded—haughty.

18. Lovers of pleasures more than lovers of God.

19. Having a form of godliness.

20. Denying the power of godliness.

Note that Paul speaks of men as being "lovers of their own selves." This is an attitude of utter selfishness and is a major characteristic of this age. Teachers must be equipped to cope with the increasing problems presented because of the prevalant attitude that personal whims and desires must be satisfied without regard to the consequences for others. The tremendous increase in crime, drug abuse, destruction of property, and other acts of unrestrained violence is a rather forceful commentary upon this selfish generation.

The word *covetous* refers to the love of money. This most certainly is a characteristic of the twentieth century. Man's love of money has led to all kinds of trouble and evil. In fact, the Bible

MOTIVATION

plainly teaches that the *love* of money is the root (foundation) of all evil. The havoc wrought because of the love of money is inestimable.

The term *boasters* used by Paul to describe last-day men is most descriptive of the world, especially so with reference to the United States. We have "boasted" of our military power, our accomplishments in space, our ability to provide the very best in medical supplies, our heroes in sports, and countless other activities to the extent that we have practically ruled out any dependence upon a higher power. This is a tremendous challenge for the Christian teacher!

The term *proud* refers to haughtiness or arrogance. This is a natural result of being lovers of our own selves, covetous, and boastful. Self-sufficient men are arrogant men. They are haughty, admitting to no need of divine guidance or provision. The teacher must realize that many or all of the pupils he teaches have been brought up from their infancy under this influence and attitude. This demands patience and understanding on the part of the teacher.

Men of the last days shall be blasphemous. A blasphemer is one who has a complete lack of reverence for God, is full of tricks (swindling), and complains violently or speaks bitterly or reproachfully. This characteristic needs no comment, as this is a most apt description of man as he is today.

Children being disobedient to parents is one of the characteristics of the last days. The rebellion of youth in this age did not happen by chance. This rebellion is dominant because we are living in the last days. Surely the Christian teacher will recognize this and prepare himself to teach these disobedient children the will, way, and purpose of the Lord for their lives.

The "unthankful attitude" spoken of needs no comment. Children are being given every desire of the heart so far as material things are concerned. Because of the affluence of our age a crop of unthankful people populate a large segment of the world today.

An unholy attitude pervades the masses. This is a great challenge to teachers. The aim of his teaching should be to cause people to pause and consider their attitude toward God, and to alter their lives so as to conform to the will of God.

Lack of natural affection characterizes the relationship between husbands and wives, parents and children of this generation. In the movies, on the television screen, in the street we are constantly reminded of the beastly lusts that pervade the world. What a challenge for the dedicated teacher.

We are living in a time when everything agreed upon must be in writing, notarized and recorded before it is accepted. After all these precautions it is common for agreements between parties to be broken without compunction. The word of man is not his bond in our generation! So it is among nations. Agreements to cease hostilities are made and broken at will. Surely we all are aware of this condition in all walks of life.

False accusers abound. For an extra dollar man will swear a lie against his neighbor. Lawsuits are common among Christians. This is in direct opposition to the teaching of the Bible according to I Corinthians 6:1-8.

Sins of the flesh flourish in our generation as never before. The masses of this age are without restraint, incontinent. Sex has become a national and international, even worldwide, god! Immorality of the lowest type pervades the printed page. People are being paid handsome sums of money for their incontinency.

The fierceness of the age is evident by the riots, lootings, murders, muggings, kidnappings, abuse of drugs, alcoholic consumption, and destruction of property rampant in all parts of the world today! The terrible sacrifice of lives in undeclared war is a result of the fierceness of this age.

Those who endeavor to live a godly life are despised as never before. The Christian is held in contempt by the majority. The

MOTIVATION

person who aspires to noble heights of Christian attainment is rejected. All this is evident as never before.

Traitors of the country are allowed to run at will unmolested in our age. Flag burners, draft dodgers, and flouters of the law are common, accepted, and even encouraged by many in places of leadership.

Reckless, willful, rash actions in the streets, colleges, homes, and schools of our world characterize this age. School administrators are in a quandary as a result of this. Law enforcement officers are intimidated and parents are bewildered. Such is the attitude confronting us today.

Haughtiness pervades the scene. An affluent generation has reached the conclusion that God is nonexistent or that if He does exist, His presence and power among men is unneeded and unwanted.

Men are certainly lovers of pleasure more than lovers of God. This has always been the attitude of unbelievers, but it is now a common and accepted attitude among those who are counted among believers, professed Christians. The pleasure seekers are determined to satisfy their lustful appetites regardless of the terrible cost attached.

It cannot be denied that there is a "form of godliness" among men today, but little power is evidenced in it. Formality, ritualism, and lack of spiritual fervor are common characteristics of the average church of this century.

What do these perilous times mean to Christian teachers? It means that as never before they are challenged to remain true to the Word of the Lord, to proclaim it with power and conviction, and in the process of doing so to hope to "save some."

Teachers who are genuinely concerned about the spiritual condition of the world in these last days are motivated to action to by all means reach some. Efforts should be redoubled because of the brevity of time for reaching man with God's message!

III. Motivated by Spiritual Ignorance Abounding Both Inside the Church and Outside It.

A. Ignorance in the Church

America is a land of churches, preachers, Christian teachers, evangelists, missionaries, and other workers in the kingdom of the Lord. Yet, spiritual ignorance is rampant today, possibly to a greater extent than ever before in the history of the acts of men. Recognition of this fact should be one of the greatest motivating forces for the dedicated teacher.

Spiritual ignorance is by no means a new thing. Paul recognized that spiritual ignorance would present a real problem to all Christian workers, and he was moved by the Holy Spirit to admonish believers concerning its influence in their lives.

1. Many Are Ignorant of the Power of Satan to Hinder.

There are so many saved people who are ignorant of the hindering force of Satan. Christians are explicitly warned of the fact that Satan can and often does hinder the most devout in his efforts in God's kingdom.

> *Now I would not have you ignorant, brethren, that oftentimes I purposed to come unto you, (but was let hitherto,) that I might have some fruit among you also, even as among other Gentiles* (Romans 1:13).

This Scripture verse should motivate the Christian teacher to put forth every effort to inform Christians of the power of Satan to hinder one in the work to which he is dedicated. Note that Paul recognized that Satan was the cause of his own unfulfilled desire (he purposed to come to them and was hindered). The power of Satan to hinder was revealed in the fact that Paul had an unaccomplished purpose (fruit among the Gentiles at Rome).

Paul reminded the Christians at Thessalonica that he had a great desire to see them face to face but did not have the privilege of then doing so.

> *Wherefore we would have come unto you, even I Paul, once and again; but Satan hindered us* (I Thessalonians 2:18).

Christian teachers must exert every effort to inform the babe in Christ that hindrances are to be expected and that they can be overcome. To so inform the young Christian is to aid them in avoiding despair when they do not succeed in every effort they put forth for the cause of Christ.

Mark relates the experience of four men who brought their palsied friend to Jesus for healing. Upon arriving at the place where the Lord was ministering, they were hindered by the multitudes surrounding Him. Their faith and determination to aid their friend led them to some rather unorthodox actions, but they did not allow the hindrances deterring them to defeat them! They resorted to the unique method of removing a portion of the roof of the house where Jesus was and through the hole in the roof they let their friend down into the room and into the presence of the Lord. The teacher likewise cannot afford to be discouraged to the point of despair and defeat when hindrances occur but rather with determination and faith in the Lord they must find a way to overcome the hindrances. Once Christian teachers have mastered the hindrances of Satan, they are in a position to tell the young converts of the secret of such success.

2. Ignorant of the Experiences of the People of the Lord

Ignorance of the people of the Lord is widespread with reference to the experiences of the people of God through the centuries. This should be a motivating factor in the life of the Christian teacher. Paul wrote to the Corinthian Christians the following:

> *... Brethren I would not that you should be ignorant, how that all our fathers were under the cloud, and all passed through the sea; And were all baptized unto Moses in the cloud and in the sea; And did all eat the same spiritual meat; And did all drink the same spiritual drink; for they drank of that spiritual Rock that followed them: and that Rock was Christ. But with many of them God was not well pleased: for they were overthrown in the wilderness. Now these things were our examples, to the intent we should not lust after evil things, as they also lusted* (I Corinthians 10:1-6).

The experiences enumerated here will serve to remind those who are saved of their relationship with and responsibility to God. The Corinthian Christians:

a. Were *directed* by the Spirit of the Lord—"Under the cloud."

b. Were *delivered* by the power of the Lord—"passed through the sea."

c. *Dined* at the table of the Lord—"did all eat the same spiritual drink; for they drank of that spiritual Rock."

The availability of these divine provisions of the Lord must be impressed upon the young convert. Blessed is the teacher who teaches that God supplies *all the needs* of His people, but more blessed is the student convert who accepts this assurance early in his

MOTIVATION

Christian experience. To be truly convinced of God's divine provisions for all things necessary is to completely rest upon God's promises. It is to accept at face value the statement of Paul to the Christians of Philippi as is recorded in Philippians 4:19:

But my God shall supply all your needs according to His riches in glory by Christ Jesus.

Paul reminded the Corinthian Christians that in spite of their relationship with the Lord, God was not well pleased with some of the Israelites and because of this displeasure many of them were overthrown in the wilderness. Christians must be taught concerning their responsibilities to God. It is imperative that the pupils be often reminded that,

... these ... were our examples, to the intent we should not lust after evil things as they also lusted.

This passage speaks of Christian responsibility as a direct result of Christian relationship with God. Though the needs of the people of the Lord were provided, He was not pleased with their conduct and as a result many never enjoyed the lifelong-awaited privilege of going into the promised land. They were overthrown in the wilderness because they lusted after the evil things of the world. The Christian teacher must make certain that he informs twentieth-century Christians of the sobering fact that these things happened to the Israelites *as an example to us!* It is a solemn and sacred duty of the Christian teacher to faithfully teach that those who lust after the things of the world will never be victorious in the Lord Jesus Christ.

The Israelites committed four grievous sins as a result of their lust. They were guilty of:

a. Ungodly worship (idolatry)

b. Unchaste conduct (fornication)

c. Unholy attitudes (tempters of Christ)

d. Unbecoming talk (murmurers)

The Christian teacher will do well to constantly remind those whom he teaches that sins, such as those enumerated above, are the direct result of lust. This, then, is why Paul admonished the Corinthians,

> *Let him that thinketh he standeth take heed lest he fall* (verse 12).

This is powerful motivation for the teacher.

3. Ignorant of the Spiritual Gifts of the Christian

There is widespread ignorance concerning the spiritual gifts the Lord has given His people. This ignorance moved Paul to write the following to the Corinthian Church:

> *Now concerning spiritual gifts, brethren, I would not have you ignorant. Ye know that ye were Gentiles, carried away unto these dumb idols, even as ye were led. Wherefore I give you to understand, that no man speaking by the Spirit of God calleth Jesus accursed: and that no man can say that Jesus is the Lord, but by the Holy Ghost. Now there are diversities of gifts but the same spirit. And there are differences of administrations, but the same Lord. And there are diversities of operations, but it is the same God which worketh all in all. But the manifestation of the Spirit is given to every man to profit withal. For to one is given by the Spirit the word of wisdom; to another the word of knowledge by the same Spirit; to another faith by the same Spirit; to another gifts of healing by the same Spirit; To another*

MOTIVATION

the working of miracles; to another prophecy; to another discerning of spirits; to another divers kinds of tongues; to another the interpretation of tongues; But all these worketh that one and the selfsame Spirit, dividing to every man severally as he will (I Corinthians 12:1-11).

The Christian teacher is in position to eradicate much of the ignorance concerning spiritual gifts that is prevalant in the church today. Because he occupies this position of importance, he must be fully equipped to teach the Bible truths concerning these gifts.

One of the most effective hindering devices of Satan is to confuse the young Christian as to what is expected of him in the accomplishment of his work as a child of God. Often, because they are ignorant of the matter, young Christians assume that they are failures as Christians when they come to the realization that they just simply do not possess the grace necessary to perform *all* the works the Holy Spirit empowers men to do. It is entirely possible that a young Christian with a great amount of zeal may embark upon a course of action even though he lacks sufficient spiritual growth in grace and maturity to reach his objective. He may have a desire to perform some work for the Lord but be totally lacking in the necessary equipment for accomplishing it. This is an indication that the Holy Spirit has not led in that direction. The victorious Christian will recognize this possibility.

The thoughtful teacher will recognize that God has not seen fit to give the nine gifts of the Spirit mentioned in the above verses to every individual. Paul was careful to point out that the *manifestation* (revelation) of the Spirit was given to *all* (verse 7) but that the specific work of the Spirit is given to those whom the Lord chooses. To one is given the qualifications for one particular work and to another is given the qualifications for an entirely different work. Yet, both these workers under the influence of the Holy Spirit can accomplish the work God called them to do, while neither of them may be able to accomplish the work of the other. *No one person is spoken of as having all the gifts of the Spirit other than the Lord Jesus Christ Himself.* The Christian teacher should be highly motivated and encouraged to aid the seeking Christian in carrying out the particular work the Lord has equipped him to do.

Before leaving this rich passage of Scripture, attention should be called to the fact that Paul declared that there are diversities of gifts, differences of administrations, and diversities of operations, but there is *only one God*. This clearly points to the fact that not only do different people have different gifts of the Spirit but that these gifts may be administered in different ways to different people. Then there are different operations of the Spirit in different people. What a consolation to know that God does not expect all Christians to obtain the same results from like efforts! Nor does He necessarily expect one individual to work or perform in the same manner as another.

4. Ignorant of Suffering for Jesus' Sake

The widespread idea that the Christian experience will eliminate all trouble and suffering from life reveals the extent of the spiritual ignorance pervading the churches of this age. The teacher should seek to expel this theory, for it has no place in Christian teaching.

> *For we would not, brethren, have you ignorant of our trouble which came to us in Asia, that we were pressed out of measure, above strength, insomuch that we despaired of life* (II Corinthians 1:8).
>
> *Yea, and all that will live godly in Christ Jesus shall suffer persecution* (II Timothy 3:12).

The above and countless other Scriptures make it abundantly clear that suffering is associated with Christianity. The wise teacher will seek to help prepare his pupils to endure the suffering as a good soldier of Jesus Christ. The suffering of Paul in Asia was so intense that he despaired of life. Though his strength was all spent, his faith in his God did not waver. This must be the attitude of the Christian of today and the teacher is challenged to teach this truth with conviction.

5. Ignorant of the Promises Concerning the Dead in Christ

But I would not have you to be ignorant, brethren, concerning them which are asleep, that ye sorrow not, even as others which have no hope (I Thessalonians 4:13).

The Christian teacher must be motivated to refute the false doctrines which some proclaim concerning the saints who die in the Lord. Paul did not want the Thessalonian Christians to be ignorant of these great truths, and surely the Christian of this age must not be ignorant of them. The death of the saints cannot be understood nor accepted with calm faith unless there is some measure of understanding concerning the glorious truths of the resurrection of Jesus, the coming of the Lord to this earth again, the appearing of the saints with Him, the rapture of the living saints, the reunion of all the saved at the coming of Jesus in the air, and the eternal presence of these saints with Jesus.

If there is any comfort to be found in this world of sin and sorrow (and there is!) it will be found in its most glorious aspect in the great truths of II Thessalonians 4:13-18. The Christian teacher will find himself stressing more and more often these great truths to those whom he teaches.

Yes, the Christian teacher will surely be motivated by the spiritual ignorance found among the saved. He will wish to teach the great Bible truths concerning the power of Satan to hinder, the experiences of God's people, the spiritual gifts for the people of the

Lord, the suffering of Christians for Jesus' sake, and the comfort a Christian can know at the time of the death of children of the Lord.

B. Ignorance Outside the Church

Needless to say, the world is filled with spiritual ignorance. Some of this ignorance is willful, some of it from false teaching, and some of it is the product of sheer indifference. The Christian teacher must be motivated to dispel this ignorance wherever possible.

1. Willful Ignorance

Peter spoke of the willful ignorance of the masses in the last days concerning the return of the Lord:

Knowing this first, that there shall come in the last days scoffers, walking after their own lusts, And saying, Where is the promise of his coming? for since the fathers fell asleep, all things continue as they were from the beginning of the creation. For this they willingly are ignorant of, that by the word of God the heavens were of old, and the earth standing out of the water and in the water: Whereby the world that then was, being overflowed with water perished: But the heavens and the earth which are now, by the same word are kept in store, reserved unto fire against the day of judgment and perdition of ungodly men. But, beloved, be not ignorant of this one thing, that one day is with the Lord as a thousand years, and a thousand years as one day. The Lord is not slack concerning his promise, as some men count slackness; but is long-suffering to us-ward, not willing that any should perish, but that all should come to repentance (II Peter 3:3-9).

MOTIVATION

It is to be noted that the root of this ignorance outside the church is in the "walking after their own lusts" described by Peter. Mid-twentieth century man is willfully ignorant of the judgments of God because he desires to be unmolested in his walk in lust. The teacher must recognize this willful ignorance if he is to effectively cope with it.

Jesus warned of this willful ignorance as He taught His disciples:

> *But as the days of No-e were, so shall also the coming of the Son of man be. For as in the days that were before the flood they were eating and drinking, marrying and giving in marriage, until the day that No-e entered into the ark, And knew not until the flood came, and took them all away; so shall also the coming of the Son of man be* (Matthew 24:37-39).

Though ignorance of impending doom was widespread in the days of Noah, it was an unnecessary ignorance. There had been ample warning and teaching, but the people remained willfully ignorant. Teachers are challenged to refute such willful ignorance in our own age!

2. Ignorance as a Result of False Teaching

Because false teachers have been common in all ages, it is imperative that Christian teachers know the truths of the Bible and that they have sufficient grace and courage to stand on and teach these great truths among those who have embraced the false doctrines. The effective teacher is not argumentative. He is not easily provoked, and will *listen* to the arguments of those who teach false doctrines. This attitude will obligate false teachers to listen to what the true teacher has to say.

There are so many who have embraced false doctrines simply because they are what they have been taught. They share in the experience of Paul, who, when speaking of his life and deeds before conversion, said that he was

> ... *before a blasphemer, and a persecuter, and injurious: but I obtained mercy, because I did it ignorantly in unbelief* (I Timothy 1:13).

Note that the apostle Paul considered that the deeds he committed against Christ were prompted by two facts: his ignorance of the fact that Jesus was the Christ, and his unbelief. Without doubt, his ignorance of the Christ resulted from erroneous teaching. The unbelief, at least in part, sprang from his spiritual ignorance. This must be recognized by the teacher of this age as the source of much indifference toward Christ on the part of those whom he teaches.

3. Ignorance in Worship

Another aspect of spiritual ignorance was mentioned by Paul from Mar's Hill:

> ... *whom, therefore ye ignorantly worship, him declare I unto you* (Acts 17:23).

The Christian teacher will come in contact with those who are ignorant of the real object of their worship. It is a real challenge for the Christian teacher to acquaint all whom he teaches with the only One worthy of worship, the one true God! The unsaved persons in the classroom present the greatest opportunity for this ministry, but there are other places and circumstances that will afford equal opportunity for introducing men to Jesus. The wise teacher will avail himself of every opportunity to dispel spiritual ignorance wherever it is found.

IV. Motivated by Unconcerned Church Members

Spiritual lethargy is sapping the church of her strength in these last days. Unconcern for the salvation of the lost and indifference concerning the stunted growth of the professing Christians characterizes the average church of this century. This attitude brings much concern to the heart of the committed Christian and is a powerful force toward more effective teaching.

Many pastors lament (and rightly so) the willful absence of many of the church members from the regular services. It is most discouraging and heartbreaking to witness the utter unconcern for the church that is shown by a large segment of the membership who consistently ignore the services and take no part in the work of the church. But church leaders must be constantly on guard lest they be more concerned about attendance than they are about the quality of instruction offered to those who *do* attend. Quality teaching is necessary to build a strong church to the glory of God.

It is entirely possible for a church to count three hundred persons in the Sunday school on a given Sunday morning while actually instructing only half that number. This is possible because 50 percent of those physically present may not be in the classrooms in spirit—their minds may be hundreds of miles away while the lesson is being taught. It is also possible that the teacher may be "hundreds of miles" off the lesson. If the pupil is not there in spirit and/or the teacher is not there in quality teaching no real teaching will be done! The possibility of these circumstances arising in the classroom should be recognized by the Christian teacher and an effort should be put forth to forestall either one.

V. Motivated by the Dedication of Many

A common mistake made by some church leaders is that of overlooking, failing to recognize, the dedication and consecration of many of the members of the church. It is indeed easy for pastors, teachers and others to allow the unfaithfulness and unconcern of many to loom so large that they become unable to see that there are yet many who do love the Lord and are committed to Him. Elijah had such an experience. In his despondency he told the Lord that he was the only one who loved Him and that it would be better if the Lord would let him die. It was then that the Lord revealed to the prophet that there were seven thousand people who had never bowed the knee to Baal. Those seven thousand loved the Lord as much as did Elijah, but they probably had not had the opportunity to express their love as had Elijah. The trouble with Elijah was that he had allowed his discouragement to blind him to the fact that these seven thousand were ready to stand with him on the Lord's side. This can and often does happen to modern church leaders. The challenge for these leaders is to look out among the people and discover those who are faithful to the cause of Christ.

Gideon probably quaked as he looked upon the 31,700 recruits for battle who turned their backs and went away because they were afraid or unfit to enter into battle for God! But he did not make the mistake of allowing this loss to convince him that defeat was certain. He turned his eyes toward that faithful 300, his heart toward God, his hand on his sword and faced the enemy. With the faithful few the battle was won. Similarly the teacher will find motivation to greater accomplishments in the few who, in spite of the many who fall away, remain steadfast and trustworthy in the battle against Satan.

4
CONSECRATION

THE CHRISTIAN TEACHER MUST NEVER PERMIT THE CUSTOMS AND DEMANDS OF THE WORLD TO INDUCE HIM TO AGREE WITH NOR CONFORM TO THE STANDARDS OF THE WORLD.

4
CONSECRATION

The successful teacher is consecrated. He is committed to Christ, to His church, and to the work he has been selected to do. He has literally accepted the challenge of Paul as it is recorded in Romans 12:1-8:

> *I beseech you therefore, brethren, by the mercies of God, that ye present your bodies a living sacrifice, holy, acceptable unto God, which is your reasonable service. And be not conformed to this world, but be ye transformed by the renewing of your mind, that ye may prove what is that good, and acceptable, and perfect, will of God. For I say, through the grace given unto me, to every man that is among you, not to think of himself more highly than he ought to think; but to think soberly, according as God has dealt to every man the measure of faith. For as we have many members in one body, and all members have not the same office: So we, being many, are one body in Christ, and every one members one of another. Having then gifts differing according to the grace that is given to us, whether prophecy, let us prophesy according to the proportion of faith; Or ministry, let us wait on our ministering: or he that teacheth, on teaching; Or he that exhorteth, on exhortation: he that giveth, let him do it with simplicity;*

he that ruleth with diligence; he that sheweth mercy, with cheerfulness.

I. A Composite Picture of the Christian Teacher

From the passage above a composite picture of the Christian, especially the Christian teacher, emerges. In this verbal description of the committed Christian we find the following attributes: 1) He recognizes the mercies of God. 2) He commits himself completely to God. 3) He does not conform to worldly standards. 4) He is transformed by continually thinking upon things that are spiritual. 5) He is a living example of Christianity in action, God's fulfilled purpose in man. 6) He is not puffed up, vainglorious, but has a sane appraisal of himself in the light of the faith God has given him. 7) He recognizes his interrelationship with others. 8) He gives himself wholly to his calling.

Recent translations are an aid in understanding Romans 12:1-8:

Phillips:

> *With eyes wide open to the mercies of God, I beg you, my brothers, as an act of intelligent worship, to give him your bodies, as a living sacrifice, consecrated to him and acceptable by him. Don't let the world around you squeeze you into its own mold, but let God remold your minds from within, so that you may prove in practice that the plan of God for you is good, meets all his demands and moves toward the goal of maturity.*
>
> *As your spiritual teacher I give this piece of advice to each of you. Do not cherish exaggerated ideas of yourself or your importance, but try to have a sane estimate of your capabilities by the light of the faith that God has given to you all. For just as you have many members in one physical body and those members differ in their*

CONSECRATION

functions, so we, though many in number, compose one body in Christ and are all members of one another. Through the grace of God we have different gifts. If our gift is preaching, let us preach to the limit of our vision. If it is serving others let us concentrate on our serving; if it is teaching let us give all we have to our teaching; and if our gift be the stimulating of the faith of others let us set ourselves to it. Let the man who is called to give, give freely; let the man who wields authority think of his responsibility; and let the man who feels sympathy for his fellows act cheerfully.

The Living Bible:

And, so, dear brothers, I plead with you to give your bodies to God. Let them be a living sacrifice, holy—the kind He can accept. When you think of what He has done for you, is this too much to ask? Don't copy the behavior and customs of this world, but be a new and different person with a fresh newness in all you do and think. Then you will learn from your own experience how His ways will really satisfy you. As God's messenger I give each of you God's warning: be honest in your estimate of yourselves, measuring your value by how much faith God has given you. Just as there are many parts to our bodies, so it is with Christ's body. We are all parts of it, and it takes every one of us to make it complete, for we each have different work to do. So we belong to each other, and each needs all the others. God has given each of us the ability to do certain things well. So if God has given you the ability to prophesy, then prophesy whenever you can—as often as your faith is strong enough to receive a message from God. If your gift is that of serving others, serve them well. If you are a teacher, do a good job of teaching. If you are a preacher, see to it that your sermons are strong and helpful. If God has given you money, be generous in helping others with it. If God has given you administrative ability and put you in charge of the work of others, take the responsibility seriously. Those who offer comfort to the sorrowing should do so with Christian cheer.

Consider the Christian teacher in the light of this passage.

A. Recognizing of the Mercies of God

Note what the apostle says:

I beseech you by the mercies of God.

Because of God's mercies the Christian teacher must give heed to the claims of the Lord upon his individual life.

He must recognize that all he is or is to be is through the mercies of God. He is anxious to give God the glory for all that is accomplished through him. He fully realizes that his eternal salvation is wholly by grace and completely unmerited by him. He acknowledges that it is by the mercies of God that he has the privilege of church membership and of occupying the place of responsibility he now fills.

B. Committing Oneself to God

The effective teacher has completely surrendered his life to the Lord. He is committed to him in body, soul, and spirit. It is worthy of note that Christians are admonished by Paul to

"... *present your bodies a living sacrifice*...."

Before the body can be presented as a living sacrifice there must of necessity be a committal of the spirit to the Lord. Note, too, that this sacrifice is *living.* The Christian does not come before his Lord with a *dead* sacrifice but rather with a living, vibrant body that is surrendered to the service of God. This is declared by Paul to be both holy and acceptable unto God.

Missionaries on a foreign field are sometimes called upon to die the death of a martyr and they do so by giving their bodies in death for the cause of Christ. The teacher of Christian truths and principles is called upon to lay down his life in sacrificial *living* for the cause of Christ. This is what is meant by a "living sacrifice."

C. Conforming to Christian Standards

Dedicated Christian teachers turn a deaf ear to the call of the world.

. . . be not conformed to this world. . . .

To be conformed to the world is to act in accordance with the rules of the world or to be in agreement with them. The Christian teacher must never permit the customs and demands of the world to induce him to agree with or conform to the standards of the world. This is true with reference to his personal or private life as well as his public life.

The Phillips translation makes the responsibility of the teacher even more personal:

Don't let the world around you squeeze you into its own mold.

The effective Christian teacher will pay particular heed to that word "let" as used in the Phillips Version. Do not *permit* the world to squeeze you into its mold. Note carefully that the responsibility for not being squeezed into the mold of the world is in the hand of the teacher. He will recognize that he will make the decision as to the course he will pursue—that of a worldly-minded person or that of a dedicated Christian.

Conformity to the world will surely undermine the good influence of the teacher. The example of the teacher in deed must speak louder than his declarations in the classroom. To obtain grace for this the teacher is driven to his knees in earnest prayer.

D. Experiencing Transformation through Spiritual Thinking

Successful teachers have been transformed. This is an experience that is absolutely necessary if one is to be the kind of teacher God will honor. To be transformed is to be changed from one power to another and this is exactly the experience of saved people. They have been changed from the power of Satan to the power of God. Note that Paul admonished the Roman Christians to

. . . be ye transformed . . .

and he immediately gave them the secret of accomplishing this:

. . . by the renewing of your mind. . . .

Thinking upon spiritual things is imperative for successful teaching.

> *As a man thinketh in his heart, so is he* (Proverbs 23:7).
>
> *Finally, brethren, whatsoever things are true, whatsoever things are honest, whatsoever things are just, whatsoever things are pure, whatsoever things are lovely, whatsoever things are of good report; if there be any virture, and if there be any praise, think on these things* (Philippians 4:8).

CONSECRATION

The Phillips translation:

> *If you believe in goodness and if you value the approval of God, fix your minds on the things which are holy and right and pure and beautiful and good.*

The Christian teacher is admonished to "renew the mind" for the following reason:

> *... that ye may prove what is that good, and acceptable, and perfect, will of God* (Romans 12:2).

The will of God for teachers is that they so teach that others will be brought into a right relationship with God.

It has been aptly stated that we have schools to inform, penal institutions to reform, but only the grace of God can transform.

E. Being a Living Example of Christianity in Action

It is imperative that the teacher of God's Word be an example of real Christianity. Note the admonition of the Phillips translation:

> *... prove in practice that the plan of God for you is good, meets all his demands and moves toward the goal of maturity.*

The teacher is under divine obligation to prove to all that God's plan is the *only good plan for his life* and to be so consistent in this attitude that others will be constrained to accept His plan for their life.

F. Maintaining a Sane Appraisal of Self

The teacher is important not because of *who* he is but rather because of *what* he is. The teacher, though he is important in the ministry of the church, must ever be mindful of the advice of Paul in verse 3:

> *Do not cherish exaggerated ideas of yourself or your importance, but try to have a sane estimate of your capabilities ...* (Phillips).

The effective teacher does not arrogantly proclaim his importance but neither does he sell himself short. He tries to see himself in the light of his capabilities as well as his limitations.

G. Recognizing the Interrelationship with Others

The Christian teacher must work in harmony with others:

> *For just as you have many members in one physical body and those members differ in their functions, so we, though many in number, compose one body in Christ and are all members of one another* (verses 4 and 5, Phillips).

There must be a right relationship existing between the various workers in the kingdom of God. Teachers must share experiences with other teachers and maintain an open line of communication between themselves and the pastor if the most effective work is to be done in the church.

H. Giving Yourself Wholly to Your Calling

The really effective teachers are those who accept the responsibility of teaching as a holy calling. This acceptance will help the teacher to give all he has to the teaching ministry. Time, talent, and energies devoted to the cause of Christ will pay dividends to the concerned teacher.

II. Attributes of the Effective Teacher

A teacher who has experienced total transformation, has been properly motivated, and makes diligent preparations has attained an unusual height of consecration. Because of his complete surrender and commitment to Christ he is in a position to use all at his command for the edifying of the body of Christ. *Consecration* is defined, "To be set apart as holy: to devote to religious use." In simple terms this means the right use of those things we possess. Note some of the possessions the Christian teacher must consecrate to God if he is to be effective:

A. Ability to Explain the Word

Effective teachers have innate abilities. These abilities must be consecrated (used rightly) if the teacher is to reach peak efficiency in his work. The ability to *explain* God's Word must be used rightly. After all, the teacher is simply explaining the Word of God and making it applicable to the lives of those whom he teaches. Not every person who *reads* God's Word is endued with the ability to *explain* it. Some may be able to read it, understand it, and feast upon it, but be wholly incapable of commanding words to explain it to others. It may be food for their souls but they do not possess the ability to feed others with it. Explaining the Word of the Lord in such a manner that others are enabled to feast upon it and receive nourishment for their spiritual lives is the work of the teacher. He should strive to excel in performing this most rewarding work.

There are those in the churches who have never learned the difference between a *noise* and a *sermon*. Many believe that if the minister makes much noise, moves about a great deal, and in general puts on a show he has *preached*. The truth of the matter is that he may not have preached at all in the real sense of preaching. His efforts may have been sincere, but unless his message was Christ-centered, Bible-related, and warmed by the fires of the Holy Spirit it was no more than a noise, or, as Paul puts it,

> *... sounding brass, or a tinkling cymbal.*

So is it concerning teaching. There are those who have not differentiated between *talking* and *teaching*. It is entirely possible for one to spend thirty or forty minutes "talking" during any given class period and yet never really teaching. The effective teacher feeds *himself* and *his class* with spiritual food from the Bible, and the results of his teaching are manifest in well-developed, balanced Christians. The teacher must use his ability to explain God's Word if he is to be successful in his efforts to teach.

B. Ability to Speak

1. Speak the Message Given of the Lord

The ability to speak is prerequisite to successful teaching. The Bible has much to say about "speaking" for the Lord. It is declared that the holy men of God:

> *... spake as they were moved by the Holy Ghost* (II Peter 1:21).

It is said that Apollos

> *... spake and taught diligently the things of the Lord* (Acts 18:25).

The Bible relates that Paul

> *... preached boldly ... in the name of the Lord Jesus* (Acts 9:27).

CONSECRATION

Those placed in the church by the Lord Jesus Christ for the edification of the church are urged to,

> ... *speak the truth in love* (Ephesians 4:15).

This presents a composite view of the responsibility of the Christian teacher to speak out. He must be moved by the Holy Spirit, diligent in declaring the Word, bold in approach, and loving in attitude.

The Christian teacher must speak out because he has an important message from the Lord. *The same Spirit that moved men to write the Bible can and will move men to declare the message of the Bible in the twentieth century.*

Effective teachers recognize their calling to

> ... *speak the things which become sound doctrine* (Titus 2:1).

Sound doctrine is derived from the Bible and the Bible is given under inspiration of the Lord. The teacher, under the unerring leadership of the Holy Spirit, is to declare this doctrine.

It is a striking fact that as the minister does not have any message to proclaim that his predecessors did not have, so the Christian teacher has nothing new to teach. He must speak for the Lord the message given him from the Bible!

2. Speak Clearly and Plainly

To be successful in teaching, the teacher must be *heard* and *understood.* Much of the inattention so prevalant in the Sunday school classes of this day would be eliminated if the teacher would speak in a manner conducive to hearing and understanding. Nothing is more boring or disinteresting than to sit under a (so-called) teacher who mumbles indistinctly and incoherently through a class period. It is no wonder that under these circumstances the class is unconcerned, disinterested, and small! The wonder is that there is a class at all who will endure this type of teaching.

It is a law of teaching that the teacher must know that which he would teach. It is also an indisputable law that, if the teacher is to be in any measure effective, he must speak so clearly that he can be heard by all in the classroom and so distinctly that he can be understood by all. Most people have probably had the experience of being in a church service when the pastor called upon some brother to lead in prayer and the brother prayed in tones so low that you "peeped" to see when the brother had completed his prayer. This is most embarrassing, is it not? It is more embarrassing to be required to sit through thirty or forty minutes of a Sunday school lesson while the teacher is mumbling incoherent mouthings that cannot be understood!

The teacher is to speak out because he has something to say, not because he has to say something. A maxim for the preacher is to stand up, speak up, and shut up! This should apply to the Christian teacher as well.

3. Speak in Love

But speaking the truth in love, may grow up into him in all things, which is the head, even Christ (Ephesians 4:15).

The ultimate goal of the Christian teacher is that he may speak in love to the extent that his hearers may grow up (mature) in Christ who is the Head of the church. It is not becoming in the Christian teacher to berate those whom he is teaching. The teacher, as an individual person, is not commissioned to reprove men of sin but rather his teaching of the Word of the Lord will accomplish this purpose. The teacher must always remember that he is subject to sins as are his pupils. Both teacher and pupil must be reproved of their sin through the Word of the Lord as it is given in the Bible. Paul made this rather clear:

> *All scripture is given by inspiration of God, and is profitable for doctrine, for reproof, for correction, for instruction in righteousness . . .* (II Timothy 3:16).

It is the duty and privilege of the teacher to point out in love that the Scriptures reprove sin. This reproof then is not of the teacher but rather of the Bible or of God.

It is imperative that the teacher learn to love the sinner while hating his sins. Love expressed in teaching will reach errant Christians as well as unsaved people much more effectively than the harsh, holier-than-thou attitude exemplified by some teachers.

4. Speak Sincerely

Believe every word you teach! This is absolutely necessary if success is to be attained. A sincere belief that the Bible is the Word of God is imperative for effective teaching. It is most necessary that the Christian teacher will not only maintain firm belief that the Bible is the Word of God, but he must also have a sincere conviction that it will, when directed by the Holy Spirit, effect a change in man. Sincerity alone is not enough, but all other attributes without sincerity are not sufficient either. Paul gives the following admonition to the Christians at Philippi:

> *. . . be sincere and without offence till the day of Christ* (Philippians 1:10).

The sincere, knowledgeable, committed, and loving teacher will not offend in his teaching.

5. Speak with Authority

These things speak, and exhort, and rebuke with all authority. Let no man despise thee (Titus 2:15).

Successful teachers speak with authority. The Phillips translation makes the above passage somewhat more meaningful to the teacher:

Tell men these things, Titus. Urge them to action, using a reprimand where necessary with all the authority of God's minister—and as such let no one treat you with contempt.

No one is to be more pitied than the Christian teacher to whom no one pays attention. However, his lack of respect may be rooted in the fact that he has not adopted a positive, knowledgeable approach in his teaching. While a teacher must never be rude, arrogant, or unfeeling, he must not be apologetic for his teaching if it is based on the Word of the Lord. He has the authority of God Himself as he teaches the truths of the Bible. Any apology for the proclamation of these truths will lead to certain contempt for the teacher.

Though the teacher is to speak with authority, this does not always assure his being right in every conclusion he reaches. The sincere teacher is receptive to the thoughts and ideas of others. In fact, the teacher often becomes the pupil and the pupil becomes the teacher. This is as it should be and will promote goodwill and a spirit of cooperation in the classroom. It is doubtful whether a teacher can be very effective if he consistently closes his mind to the thoughts of others.

The personal life of the teacher inside and outside the classroom will determine, to a great extent, the respect he will receive from those whom he teaches. Action speaks more eloquently than words, and this is especially true with reference to the Christian teacher. The life lived among his people must be consistent with the teaching

CONSECRATION

of the Bible or the teacher is apt to be held in contempt. Successful teaching demands that the teacher avoid contempt at all costs.

6. Speak Often (Regularly)

The effective teacher speaks often and regularly! He loves his Lord, his church, his class, his Bible, and his office to such an extent that he will regularly fill his own place of responsibility. A good teacher is not constantly looking for excuses to be away from his post of duty. He is always seeking the opportunity to show his love by attending the services of the church and by being prepared to teach every week.

The teacher who forms the habit of being absent from his class often is apt to have a class composed of pupils who will also be away often. The teacher is obligated under God to set the example in faithfulness. Unless hindered by circumstances beyond his control, there are few reasons why a teacher should be absent from his post of duty.

The teacher who sets as his goal a record of perfect attendance and encourages the members of the class to do likewise is apt to develop a class of interested and concerned members.

7. Speak with Expectation

He that goeth forth and weepeth, bearing precious seed, shall doubtless come again with rejoicing, bringing his sheaves with him (Psalm 126:6).

The psalmist outlined the Christian worker's position. Note that he speaks of "going forth," which indicates that he does not consider it too great a sacrifice to go where the Lord demands. Surely the Christian teacher is obligated to "go" to the house of the Lord to discharge his responsibility as a teacher. David mentioned the fact that the "going" was to be accompanied by "weeping." This speaks of a deep concern on the part of the Christian. Next in order is the fact that he is to bear "precious seed," which refers to the teacher's declaration of the Word of the Lord. Having gone forth with weeping, bearing the precious Word of the Lord, the teacher can expect to "come again [return] with rejoicing" and to bring "his sheaves," the reward of his efforts, with him.

The Christian teacher has every reason for speaking with expectation because the fields in which he works are indeed white unto harvest. He can reasonably expect to see the salvation of souls and spiritual development of those who are saved.

The importance of speaking clearly and plainly in the teaching ministry is succinctly pointed out in Nehemiah 8:8:

So they read in the book in the law of God distinctly, and gave the sense, and caused them to understand the reading.

Here is the teacher's guide to effective teaching. Note that:

a. They read the book of the law. God's book was their textbook just as the Bible is the only textbook for Christian teachers of this generation. The Bible is our all-sufficient rule of faith and conduct and is consequently the only textbook the teacher is authorized to teach.

b. *They read distinctly.* These men of God read from the book of the Lord in such a manner that the audience could hear and understand the reading. The Christian teacher must always read loudly enough to be heard and clearly enough to be understood if he is to be effective in presenting the message of the Lord.

c. *They gave the sense.* Reading, though it may be done ever so distinctly, is not all the teacher is to do. He is to give the sense of the reading. Most people can read the Bible but multitudes are not able to determine what it really means. This is one great work and challenge of the teacher—he must be able to *explain* the message of the Bible.

d. *They caused them to understand.* This is the ultimate goal of the teacher. Causing the people who *hear* to *understand* the message is often no small task. Jesus often alluded to this fact:

> *"He that hath an ear let him hear what the Spirit saith unto the churches."*

The teacher must never be satisifed until he has succeeded in causing his hearers to understand.

The word *understand* as used in Nehemiah 8:8 means "to separate mentally" or "to distinguish." The teacher's work is to aid the hearer in separating the message of the Lord from that of the world, the truth of the Bible from traditions of man. He is to lead his people into such knowledge of spiritual things that they are enabled to distinguish between the things of God and those of Satan.

e. *Ability to command respect.* One more trait is implied, although not precisely stated. The teachers who read God's law under Ezra's guidance commanded the respect of the people they taught. No teacher will succeed if he does not have the respect of those whom he endeavors to teach. People in all walks of life usually receive the respect they deserve!

To command respect requires some sacrifices. It also requires self-discipline. Paul referred to the fact:

> *... I keep under my body, and bring it into subjection: lest that by any means, when I have preached to others, I myself should be a castaway* (I Corinthians 9:27).

The Revised Standard Version:

> *But I pommel my body and subdue it, lest after preaching to others I myself should be disqualified.*

Phillips:

> *I am my body's sternest master, for fear that when I have preached to others I should myself be disqualified.*

The New English Bible:

> *I bruise my own body and make it know its master, for fear that after preaching to others I should find myself rejected.*

The Amplified Bible:

> *But I buffet my body—handle it roughly, discipline it by hardships—and subdue it, for fear that after proclaiming to others the Gospel, and things pertaining to it, I myself should become unfit—not stand the test and be unapproved—and rejected.*

These five versions of the Bible use five different terms to describe the Christian teacher who, because he lacks self-discipline, fails to command the respect of those to whom he ministers. Note that he is:

- —a castaway
- —disqualified
- —rejected
- —unfit
- —unapproved

It is imperative that the teacher of the Word of God so live that his life will be an example of Christianity in action.

5
PREPARATION

THE MIND OF MAN,
AS IT IS BY NATURE,
WILL NEVER BE ABLE TO GRASP
THE DEEP TRUTHS OF THE LORD,
NOR WILL IT EVER BY NATURE
BE QUALIFIED TO PASS
THESE GREAT TRUTHS ON TO OTHERS.

5
PREPARATION

If any of you lack wisdom, let him ask of God, that giveth to all men liberally, and upbraideth not; and it shall be given him (James 1:5).

Every truly Christian teacher will voluntarily place himself in company with those who lack wisdom. He realizes his utter inability to effectively teach God's Word without divine aid. He recognizes that the task is far too great for man alone. In order to assume the tremendous responsibility of teaching he must seek help from above. This is the first step in preparing for really effective teaching.

I. Preparation through Prayer

The teacher has much to pray about and much to pray for. Effective teaching demands fervency in prayer.

A. Pray for Divine Aid in Understanding the Lesson to Be Taught

... the carnal mind is enmity against God: for it is not subject to the law of God, neither indeed can be (Romans 8:7).

The mind of man, as it is by nature, will never be able to grasp the deep truths of the Lord, nor will it ever by nature be qualified to pass these great truths on to others! Paul clearly states that the carnal mind is an enemy of God. The teacher must not depend on the carnal mind to reveal the Word of the Lord to him. Since the carnal mind does not possess this wisdom, the teacher who would succeed must accept the advice and challenge of James to

> ... *ask of God who giveth ... liberally.* ...

One of the cardinal laws of teaching is that the teacher must know that which he would teach. The only way the teacher's mind can be prepared to learn the truths of the Bible is through the divine aid of the Holy Spirit. If one would know the Bible, he must submit himself to the leading and teaching of the Holy Spirit. Prayer is an absolute imperative for the attainment of this attitude.

B. Pray for Divine Guidance in Presentation of the Lesson.

It is not sufficient that the teacher just know the material—he must be able to present the material in such a manner that the end result of his teaching will be enlightened hearers. Teaching has not actually been accomplished until there has been learning on the part of the pupil. Though the teacher may have great knowledge of the subject matter, his teaching becomes effective only as those who hear are able to grasp the truths presented.

There are several proven methods of lesson presentation. Among these are lecture, discussion, question and answer, research, story telling, and recitation. Although each of these methods is good and can be used most effectively, it is the responsibility of the teacher to determine which of the various methods is best suited for a *particular* lesson and for a particular group.

The presentation of the lesson should by all means be interesting. Interesting lesson presentation does not require that the teacher

PREPARATION

spend his time in telling jokes. Good illustrations, some relevant current event, proper use of object lessons, facial expressions and gestures are just a few of the available means of making the lesson interesting.

The truly concerned teacher will not hesitate to ask the Lord to give him the necessary means of presenting an interesting lesson. Interesting lesson presentation usually means attentive pupils and attentive pupils are learning pupils. Learning pupils are maturing pupils and maturing pupils are tomorrow's effective teachers. Thus the cycle starts all over again. The effective teacher continues to live in succeeding generations of teachers.

The Christian teacher must make the lesson relevant to the needs of his pupils. While there is not an irrevelant word in the Bible, it is nevertheless a fact that the lesson must be related to the lives of those being taught. We hear a great deal about relevancy in our time and many have taken the position that the Bible is not relevant to the problems of this age. The Bible *is* relevant to this age. The teacher is challenged to seek out the relevancy and make it plain to the pupils.

One might ask how the account of the flood which occurred more than four thousand years ago could possibly be relevant to the twentieth century. The answer is simple; judgment for sin came upon the world in the flood. Today, four thousand years later, we are under the power of the same God and men are sinning in the same manner in which the antediluvians sinned. God has not changed; man has not changed. Therefore the account of the flood is relevant to the twentieth century because it teaches the dire consequences of rejecting God's commandments.

Every Bible event is somehow relevant to the needs of man. It is the responsibility of the teacher to pray for divine guidance in presenting the Word in order that this relevancy may be made evident.

C. Pray for the Pupils Being Taught

The successful teacher has a genuine interest in the pupils whom he teaches. He is keenly aware of their individual importance. He is anxious to bring the lost to a saving knowledge of Christ and to see the saved develop into stalwart, mature Christians. He desires that each will have a close fellowship with the Lord.

Teachers who face reality also recognize that there are many obstacles to overcome if the pupil is to attain the goals desired. There are circumstances at home, at school, at work, and at play that hinder the lost from accepting Christ and the saved from a full and complete surrender to the will of the Lord. The efficient teacher does not sit in judgment but rather with a deep compassion prays for the individuals so hindered.

Knowing some of the circumstances under which a person lives enables one to more effectively teach that person. It would be well for the teacher to evaluate each of his pupils. Some of the questions he would wish to consider are:

1. Is the pupil intelligent or dull?

2. Is the pupil industrious or lazy?

3. Is he respectful or disrespectful?

4. Is he concerned or unconcerned?

5. Is he courteous or discourteous?

6. Is he polite or impolite?

7. Is he quiet or boisterous?

Questions bearing upon his homelife which might offer an insight into his progress are:

1. Is the pupil from a religious or irreligious home?

2. Is he from a poverty stricken, average, or well-to-do home?

3. Does he come from a happy home?

4. Has he been disciplined at home?

5. Does he have a background of spiritual teaching and training?

6. Does he attend classes because of a sense of responsibility to the church?

7. Is his real purpose in attending to better equip himself to serve the Lord?

These and other questions concerning the pupil should be considered by the teacher as he makes preparation to teach. Knowing as far as possible the answers to these questions will enable the teacher to prepare his lesson in such a manner that many obstacles will be overcome and the pupil will gain a better knowledge of the Word of the Lord.

II. Preparation through Study

Study to shew thyself approved unto God, a workman that needeth not to be ashamed, rightly dividing the word of truth (II Timothy 2:15).

The watchword of the teacher is "study." There is no substitute for this. Timothy was commanded to study for some most specific reasons. What are they?

Study to show thyself approved unto God....

Note that the approval of *God* is to be sought, not that of man. The successful teacher is concerned with the approbation of the Lord rather than that of man! Too often, the opposite is the rule. Man is prone to be preoccupied with how he may please man. Paul advised Timothy to study in order that he might show others, those to whom he ministered, that he was approved of the Lord in the work he was doing. One should apply himself to acquiring knowledge with which the Lord will be pleased.

Study to show thyself . . . a workman. . . .

The teacher is not only concerned with the approval of the Lord but he is to seek out ways and means of giving evidence that he is a *workman. Strong's Exhaustive Concordance* indicates that the word "workman" could well be rendered "teacher." Study to show thyself a *teacher!* He who occupies the position of a teacher is under divine obligation to prove that he in fact is such. What does it mean to *teach?* It has been defined "to show how to do something; give instructions to; train. . . ."

A teacher should ask himself if he meets the requirements of teaching as defined above. Is he really qualified to show others how to do something? In the case of a Christian teacher this would involve his *conduct* fully as much as his words. His life and conduct must show others how to live as a Christian. The really effective teacher's life and conduct shows true humility, repentance for sin, compassion for others—in short, he is an example to the world.

To teach is to give instructions. This involves superior knowledge. If the pupils of the class were as well instructed and as well acquainted with the subject material as the teacher, it would be impossible to have a teaching situation. The teacher, then is to not only be able to set an example in Christian living but he is to be able to *tell* others the way of the Lord.

Training is involved in teaching. Pouring knowledge into the head of a student is not all there is to teaching. The student must be trained to use the knowledge he gains from study. The successful teacher is not satisfied until the student has acquired skill in the use of the knowledge he has acquired.

Study to show thyself . . . not ashamed.

PREPARATION

The successful teacher is never boastful of his accomplishments. Nevertheless, he is not ashamed of them. The measure of the success of the teacher is the life of the pupil who has been taught. There is no greater satisfaction than knowing that those who are taught are practicing what they were taught. This is exactly what John was referring to when he stated,

I have no greater joy than to hear that my children walk in the truth (III John 4).

The joy of the Christian teacher is to know that those whom he has taught are *walking in the truth.* This is the ultimate goal of every effective teacher.

Another point to be born in mind by the teacher is that he is to study in order that he may not be ashamed of his preparation and presentation of the lesson. To endeavor to teach without proper preparation is to invite circumstances that cause one to be "ashamed." If the teacher refuses to make proper preparation he will be ashamed of the presentation of his unprepared lesson, as well he should be. Work carelessly done is work of which one is apt to be ashamed. There is no place for unprepared teachers among those who are not ashamed of their teaching.

Study to show thyself . . . rightly dividing the word of truth.

The teacher is under obligation to his Lord to *rightly divide* the word of truth. We are told that the word *divide* means to "make a straight cut." This indicates that the teacher is not at liberty to deviate in any way from the Word. The *truth* must be taught regardless of whom it will please or displease. It is important that the teacher remember that he is to *rightly* "make a straight cut." God has given the textbook and charged the teacher with the responsibility of teaching only that which is found therein.

The admonition has been given to the teacher to study. The reasons for study have been enumerated. The question logically arises as to what the teacher is to study. There are several things that the effective teacher must study.

A. Study the Bible

It is obvious that effective teachers study the Bible since this is the only textbook of the Christian teacher. Read what Paul wrote to Timothy:

> *All Scripture is given by inspiration of God, and is profitable for doctrine, for reproof, for correction, for instruction in righteousness: That the man of God may be perfect, thoroughly furnished unto all good works* (II Timothy 3:16-17).

1. Study the Scriptures to Be Effective

The study of the Scriptures is an absolute imperative if the Christian teacher is to approach effectiveness. It is to be noted that Paul declares the Scriptures to be profitable for

a. Doctrine, which is *teaching*.

b. Reproof, which is rebuke or censure.

c. Correction, which is changing from wrong to right.

d. Instruction in righteousness, which is teaching how to live the godly life.

The Christian teacher is most assuredly involved in the teaching of doctrine. Those who assert that they do not appreciate doctrinal teaching are declaring that they do not appreciate Bible teaching, for the Bible is a doctrinal book from Genesis through Revelation. A simple definition of *doctrine* is "something taught." The Bible was given that man might be taught of God and His relationship with men.

2. Study the Bible in Order to Tell Others the Way of Salvation

Timothy was admonished by Paul to remember that

> ... *from a child thou hast known the holy scriptures, which are able to make thee wise unto salvation through faith which is in Christ Jesus* (II Timothy 3:15).

This Scripture sets before us another imperative reason why the Christian teacher must diligently study the Bible. The Bible is the only book that reveals the way of salvation to sinning man, and Christian teachers are vitally concerned with sinners and salvation. Salvation through Christ is a *doctrinal* truth.

3. Study the Bible to Obtain Spiritual Nourishment for Yourself

A third good reason for the teacher to study the Bible is that it is food for his own soul. The church at Corinth was chided by Paul because he was forced to feed them "milk" rather than "meat." The Bible contains milk for the infant and infirm and meat for the stalwart, fully-developed Christian. The teacher has experienced a most definite need for both "milk" and "meat" in his own spiritual life, and he will do well to determine the need of those in his class whom he teaches before he sets out to "feed" them upon the Word of the Lord. But whether the Word taught is "milk" or "meat," it is doctrinal and should be accepted by both pupil and teacher as God's message.

4. Study the Bible that It May Become a Safeguard against Sinning against God

Thy Word have I hid in mine heart, that I might not sin against thee (Psalm 119:11).

Hiding the Word of the Lord in the heart is the Christian's surest way of staying close to the Lord. The hidden Word in the heart will teach the teacher how to live as a Christian and how to teach as a teacher.

5. Study the Bible in Order to Be Enabled to Bring Out Its Reproving Power of Sin

The Word of the Lord, rather than the teacher as such, must reprove sinners. The teacher, subject to sin himself, is mortal, he is finite. Because of this fact, the teacher stands in the presence of God as others do—a sinner by nature.

Because man is a sinner by nature, it is necessary that he have something other than his personal experiences and conduct with which he may reprove sin. This reproof is furnished by the Bible, and the Bible only. The Bible reproves sin in the life of the pupil and it reproves sin in the life of the teacher. God's Word reproves sin wherever sin is found.

6. Study the Bible that You May Offer a Corrective Course of Action

The Christian teacher must study the Bible if he is to instruct individuals in righteousness. Righteousness is the very opposite of sinfulness. By nature, man knows how to live *sinfully*. But, man must be taught from the Bible how to live *righteously*. The responsibility of the teacher is to seek out God's truths and principles and to

PREPARATION

instruct others in them. Surely the Christian teacher will recognize that it is absolutely imperative that he give himself to a study of the Word of the Lord if he is to instruct others in it.

B. Study Various Teaching Aids

There are a few people who object to the use of literature in the teaching ministry of the church. Why they do so is beyond the comprehension of this writer. Certainly literature is no new thing for use by Christian teachers and other workers of the church. Paul wrote to Timothy:

> ... *when thou comest, bring with thee ... the books, but especially the parchments* (II Timothy 4:13).

Books and parchments—literature—were used by the apostle Paul and they should be utilized today if the teacher is to succeed in his work.

Literature worthy to be used in Christian teaching is Bible oriented and Christ centered. No other kind of literature will suffice for the Christian teacher. The teacher will do well to study the lesson thoroughly in the Bible before considering the comments in the various commentaries, including that of the quarterly. Having studied the Bible, the teacher can then turn to other teaching aids to aid him in understanding what is to be taught.

Literature must never take the place of the Bible! It was never intended for that purpose and to use it in such a manner is to defeat its purpose. Literature is an *aid* to Bible study. *The teacher who teaches literature is making a fatal teaching error.* Literature was never intended as a Sunday school textbook. The Bible is the textbook from which all effective teachers teach. *Literature is intended to be used in the home as an aid to understanding the lesson to be taught.* It would be well if the Bible were so studied and the literature so utilized in the home that there would be no need for literature in the classroom of the church.

The effective teacher will take advantage of the help to be obtained from good literature but will never allow the quarterly or any other literature to become his textbook in the classroom.

There are other helps the teacher will wish to utilize in the preparation of the lesson material for teaching. Among the helps most needed will be a good Bible atlas, a Bible dictionary, a good concordance, and certainly one or more commentaries that are true to the Bible.

The effective teacher will not hesitate to use material which has been gleaned from the efforts of others who have given their talents and energies in searching out the truths of the Bible. No teacher can be completely original in his thinking.

C. Study Your Pupils

It is absolutely necessary that the teacher know his pupils if he is to be successful in teaching them. In order to know the pupils, the teacher must study them diligently and under varying circumstances. There are many things that the teacher should know about those whom he teaches.

The successful teacher will know his pupils to the extent that he has determined something about their capacity to learn. One of the tragic mistakes often made in the classroom is the pupil being ridiculed because he does not happen to know the answer to some question though the question be ever so elementary. The wise teacher will never permit a pupil to be ridiculed under any circumstances. In order to effectively prevent this from happening, the teacher must know the learning capacity of each of his pupils *and he must respect that capacity* regardless of the knowledge or lack of knowledge exemplified by the student.

Know your students well enough to anticipate some of the

questions in their minds. Not every question is spoken. Many questions can be read in the expression of the pupil, his eyes or his actions may speak more eloquently than words. Be prepared to anticipate those unspoken questions and answer them though they are unspoken. The unspoken questions are usually the most important ones and should never be ignored.

For effective teaching, study your Bible to know what God has to say on the subject. Study your literature to determine what dedicated scholarship has gleaned from the Word of the Lord. Study your teaching methods in order that you may more effectively present the truths of God's Word to those whom you teach.

III. Preparation through Teacher Improvement Programs

No teacher is 100 percent effective. No teacher has learned all there is to be learned about the Bible. Because of this, there is room for improvement among all those who teach. The truly concerned teacher will wish to take advantage of every teacher improvement program available to him. There are several programs available which will be of great benefit to the teacher in his teaching ministry.

A. Teachers' and Officers' meetings

Every church should maintain a regular (preferably weekly) meeting for teachers and officers. This can truly be a blessing to the teaching ministry of the church if it is conducted in such a manner that the potential may be reached. This meeting is not a social for church workers. Socials for the workers are good and proper in their right place but the regular meeting for officers and teachers *must be set aside as a time of mutual sharing of ideas, fervent praying for spiritual power, diligent study of the lesson to be taught, frank discussion of the problems faced, and honest appraisal of the results obtained in the teaching ministry.*

Whatever period of time is designated for this important meeting should be time dedicated for that purpose and the pastor and other leaders of the church should let it be known that those who will teach are expected to attend.

By sharing ideas the teachers have access to approaches used by others in the teaching ministry. Variety in teaching makes for interested pupils and it is well for the teachers to discuss their teaching procedure and to adapt the various methods that have proven effective for others.

Some of the time set aside for the weekly meeting of the workers of the church should be devoted to a discussion of the following Sunday's lesson. It is here that teachers can come to agreement as to the meaning of obscure or difficult passages and thus assure unified teaching in each of the classrooms.

Any peculiar problems or difficulties encountered in the teaching ministry should be frankly discussed in these meetings. Every Christian teacher encounters problems. Some of the problems arise due to the conduct of a member or members of the class. The wise teacher will not hesitate to seek counsel and guidance from others concerning how to handle these problem pupils. Many times the teacher is surprised to learn that some other teacher has encountered the same problem and has effectively solved it. Sharing this information can make the difference between effective and ineffective teaching.

Another problem often encountered by the Christian teacher is that of gaining and holding the attention of the class. Sometimes the root of this problem is traced to the teacher himself. The sincere teacher will not resent others probing into his teaching methods if he is constantly having difficulty in maintaining the attention of his class. Mannerisms of which the teacher is completely unaware may be distracting to his class. His teaching method may be inappropriate for the age group or his tone of voice may be unsuitable. Lack of organization on the part of the teacher leads to confusion in the minds of the pupils. Lack of preparation for the presentation of the lesson will always result in a lack of attention on the part of the pupils.

Other problems encountered by the teacher are the result of lack of real concern and wise planning on the part of the church. The church that would have a strong teaching ministry must provide necessary equipment and facilities for effective work on the part of the teachers. A comfortable place of meeting must be provided. This will require well-regulated heat and air as well as chairs, tables, and other furniture for the classroom.

Ample Christ-centered, Bible-oriented literature must be available to the teacher, as well as maps, charts, visual aids, and chalk boards for his use in gaining and holding the attention of the class.

The lack of any of these teaching aids should be candidly discussed in teachers' and officers' meetings and recommendations concerning them should be made by this group to the proper church committee. Soldiers are not sent into battle against the enemy without proper equipment; neither should the church expect her teachers to be effective in their work unless every effort is made to provide necessary equipment for their use.

B. Parent-Teacher Organization

Active Parent-Teacher Associations in the public schools have long been encouraged because school administrators and teachers have learned the value of communication with the parents of those whom they teach. The same principle could prove a real blessing to the teaching ministry of the church. Occasional meetings between the teachers and the parents of the pupils could well be the means of finding solutions to some of the problems encountered in teaching. The spiritual progress, or lack of it as the case may be, should be the main topic of discussion in these meetings. Candid discussions on the part of both teacher and parent will be the key to the success of such a meeting. If this type of organization is to fulfill its purpose there must be no bias, no making of excuses, no covering the problems—only a frank admission of difficulties and an honest search for the solution to them.

If the attitude of a pupil is such that he becomes a disruptive factor in the classroom the teacher should be prepared to candidly discuss this with the parents. The parents should be willing to face reality and with the help of the teacher map out a cooperative plan of action that is conducive to learning. This plan should be designed to help the student to understand the importance of behavior in the classroom.

C. Planning Sessions

Planning sessions with the pastor and superintendent should be held regularly. Coordination of the teachers' efforts can be of great benefit to the teaching ministry and during these sessions long-range plans can be made. A survey of the lessons for the year should be made and plans laid out for the effective presentation of them in each classroom. Attendance campaigns, spiritual development emphasis, and other promotional efforts should be planned as the pastor, the superintendent, and the teachers reach mutual agreement as to the time best suited for these programs.

The pastor, superintendent, and teachers form an ideal group for perfecting plans for promoting an annual workers' banquet. This can be one of the most rewarding activities among those who are chosen to work in any capacity in the church. The time and place of meeting and the speaker for the occasion should be selected well in advance in order that all workers of the church will have ample time to make the necessary arrangements to attend. It is recommended that this banquet be held at some place other than the church. The expenses are usually paid by those attending but some churches bear the expense. The cost involved is insignificant when compared with the results it obtains through a better relationship among those chosen to work in official capacities in the church.

D. Clinics and Study Courses

Every church should conduct at least one clinic and one study course each year for its workers. Clinics provide opportunity for teachers and other workers to take an inventory and determine the gains or losses, while the study courses will offer them opportunities for improvement in teaching.

A person not feeling well will go to the doctor (clinic) and there he will be examined, a diagnosis will be made, and a prescription offered to affect a cure. This is exactly what teaching clinics should strive to do for the teaching ministry. If the teaching ministry is not up to par it will pay dividends for the church to undergo a critical examination to determine what the problems are (diagnosis), then search for an effective means of overcoming them (cure). This all sounds very easy as we look at it on paper, but as the medical doctor is often baffled by the symptoms of disease and finds it most difficult to make a diagnosis, so it is often difficult to know exactly what is the malady of the teaching ministry. Until the malady is determined no successful treatment can be prescribed to affect a cure. The clinic can do much toward determining the disease and offering a cure.

Study courses should be encouraged in each church. Public school teachers are required to meet certain academic standards before they are qualified to teach and in order to meet those requirements they must periodically attend classes which specialize in teaching them the newest techniques of teaching. Even so should the Christian teacher be provided specialized classes in which he can learn of the most effective techniques for teaching his pupils the Word of the Lord. There are many good textbooks for such study courses and the church should make them available to all teachers in regular yearly or biyearly study courses.

Area clinics and study courses are usually available to teachers in addition to those conducted by the local church. Usually a number of churches in a given area will cooperate in a joint effort. This is especially effective in an area where most of the churches are small. These churches can pool their resources to procure qualified workers for these clinics or study courses and receive the same benefits as those larger churches who have their own teacher improvement program.

e. Various Books on Teaching

The alert teacher reads much. Among the books he will read will be some dealing with mechanics of teaching as well as those intended to inspire the teacher. Churches should provide a library for the use of the teaching staff. This library should contain the latest books on effective teaching and the teachers should study them to obtain help in accomplishing the work they have been called upon to do.

6
PRESENTATION

ENERGETIC PREPARATION
PLUS ENERGETIC PRESENTATION
WILL EQUAL SUCCESS
IN THE TEACHING MINISTRY
IF OTHER REQUIREMENTS ARE MET
BY THE CHRISTIAN TEACHER.

6
PRESENTATION

It is possible for a teacher to recognize and accept the challenge of teaching, to be highly motivated to teach, and to make diligent preparation for this work and yet not succeed as a teacher. There is at least one other necessary ingredient for effective teaching, and that is *presentation of the material.* The successful teacher is forceful and enthusiastic and presents the lesson in an interesting manner. If he is lacking in these qualities, regardless of the time and energy expended in preparation prior to classtime, he cannot possibly reach peak efficiency in teaching.

I. The Teacher Must Be Forceful

To be forceful in the presentation of lesson material the teacher must possess and cultivate certain personal qualities.

A. Full of Force

The successful teacher so teaches that the hearers are caused to act or move as a result of the teaching, even though this action or moving may not be the intention of the hearer. Good teaching over a period of time will exert an influence over even the most callous hearers.

Forceful teaching concerning the death, burial, and resurrection of Jesus will have its effect upon the unsaved. Not all people who are saved are reached from the pulpit. Many lost people have found Jesus as a personal Saviour as the result of forceful teaching in the classroom. Actually, forceful teaching coupled with Bible preaching is a combination God uses most often to awaken a sinner to his condition. This once again calls attention to the fact that the *teacher* and the *preacher* are a Scriptural team. When they work together in oneness of purpose the result will be the salvation of souls.

The backslidden child of God will be moved by forceful teaching. While it is a primary function of the church to win souls to the Lord and the teacher plays a most important role in the accomplishment of this work, it must be remembered that those who are saved must be taught concerning the Christian life. Because the church sometimes ignores her responsibility to teach young converts, there is a great number of backsliders among us. The successful church is the church whose members have been taught from the Bible how to live the godly life. The teacher should be encouraged to give attention to the *teaching* of the saved as well as to the *reaching* of the lost.

Yes, the most hardened sinner and the most backslidden child of God can be moved by the sheer force of Bible teaching. Though it is not the force of the teacher but rather the force of the Word of the Lord that moves people to right action, it nevertheless is most important that the teacher present the message of the Bible with all the power of his personality.

B. Vigorous

The successful teacher is not indolent. Preparation for teaching and presentation of materials demands energy. Energetic preparation is useless unless presentation is made with vigor. Energetic preparation plus energetic presentation will equal success in the teaching ministry if other requirements are met by the Christian teacher.

The work of teaching will become a monotonous grind and a drain upon the teacher both physically and mentally unless the teacher is renewed day by day through the power of the Holy Spirit. Paul spoke of the exertion required for effective service to the Lord:

We having the same spirit of faith, according as it is written, I believed, and therefore have spoken; we also believe, and therefore speak; Knowing that he which raised up the Lord Jesus shall raise up us also by Jesus, and shall present us with you. For all things are for your sakes, that the abundant grace might through the thanksgiving of many redound to the glory of God. For which cause we faint not; but though our outward man perish, yet the inward man is renewed day by day. For our light affliction, which is but for a moment, worketh for us a far more exceeding and eternal weight of glory; While we look not at the things which are seen, but at the things which are not seen: for the things which are seen are temporal; but the things which are not seen are eternal (II Corinthians 4:13-18).

Note that Paul declared that he fainted not because the thanksgiving of many, as a result of his efforts, brought glory to God. Energetic service will not only bring honor to God but as Paul stated,

... *though our outward man perish, yet the inward man is renewed day by day.*

Teaching that is effective will energize the teacher for ever greater efforts.

It should be noted, too, that Paul quoted the psalmist:

I believed, and therefore have I spoken;

Paul added,

we also believe and therefore speak.

The psalmist's declarations were prompted by an inner conviction. Paul declared that he, too, spoke only after he had believed. The effective teacher *believes* what he teaches. To do less than believe that which one teaches is to be hypocritical and thus ineffective.

The matter of believing what one teaches is most important. Effective teaching demands that the teacher present the lessons with the conviction that his teaching is truth. It is not sufficient for the teacher to teach what others believe. He must believe and therefore speak. Teaching based upon the conviction that what is taught is truth and will result in bringing glory to God will give to the teacher the experience of daily renewal. This, as nothing else, will give force to Bible teaching.

C. Cogent

Effective teaching will exert a powerful influence upon the mind of the hearers. Teachers who are successful do not teach just in order to be heard or to hear themselves but rather with a view to persuasion. They expect their teaching to influence the thinking of those taught. They should utilize every means available to appeal to the mind of those who are taught.

Cogency in teaching will compel some to change their minds and their attitudes. It often drives the unbeliever to discard his unbelief and place his trust in Christ as his Saviour. It will move the erring saint to a closer relationship with his Lord. It will convince the skeptical of the claims of the Lord upon his life.

In order to teach cogently the teacher must speak with clarity. He must speak so clearly that every word he speaks can be heard and so plainly that everything he says is understood by those who hear him. The teacher who uses words and phrases that are unfamiliar to the hearers will never attain success as a teacher. Likewise, the teacher who mutters or mumbles throughout a class period has failed to teach. Nothing is more tiring or boring than a thirty- or forty-minute class period in which the teacher's words can either not be heard or understood! About all the pupils in that class will learn is to shun that class. Not all the absenteeism in the Sunday school is the fault of the student. Some, probably a greater amount than is acknowledged, is traceable to the person charged with the solemn responsibility of teaching.

II. The Teacher Must Be Enthusiastic

The original meaning of the word *enthusiasm* was "to be supernaturally inspired." This original meaning should be applied with reference to the Christian teacher. It does not violate Scripture to say that one can be and is inspired of the Lord in this age. On the contrary it is most tragic to witness the results of the efforts of teachers who do not have this inspiration. Jesus spoke of this when He was comforting His disciples immediately preceding His crucifixion:

> *Howbeit when he, the Spirit of truth, is come, he will guide you into all truth: for he shall not speak of himself; but whatsoever he shall hear, that shall he speak: and he will shew you things to come. He shall glorify me: for he shall receive of mine, and shall shew it unto you* (John 16:13-14).

This work of the Spirit has not been annulled. He is at work today guiding those who will hear to the truths they should know. He is revealing truths that have hitherto been unknown by them. Enthusiasm or supernatural inspiration is noted in the following Scriptural references:

A. Inspired Scripture Is the Teacher's Textbook

> *All scripture is given by inspiration of God, and is profitable for doctrine, for reproof, for correction, for*

instruction in righteousness: That the man of God may be perfect, thoroughly furnished unto all good works (II Timothy 3:16-17).

Though the teacher will find much supplemental material to assist him in teaching God's Word, there remains only one *textbook* for the effective teacher. That book is the Bible. All other writing must fade into utter insignificance when compared with the inspired Word of the Lord.

B. Inspired Study Is the Teacher's Command

Study to shew thyself approved unto God, a workman that needeth not to be ashamed, rightly dividing the word of truth (II Timothy 2:15).

The teacher who becomes enthused over studying the Bible in order to obtain its message for himself first and then to pass this knowledge along to others is a happy teacher. It should ever be born in mind that one must study to show himself approved unto God—not necessarily unto man. The workman (teacher) that would not be ashamed is the workman who has rightly divided (driven a straight furrow in his teaching of) the Word of Truth.

Study is the act or process of applying the mind in order to acquire knowledge. There is no real Bible knowledge that has not been acquired through personal application of one's mind to the acquiring of that knowledge. This simply points out the fact that all teaching is not necessarily truth. The effective teacher first applies his mind to acquire knowledge of the Bible, then insists upon the same course of procedure for those whom he teaches. Successful teachers have no fear of having their teaching tested by the searching of the Bible to determine that it is true to the Bible.

There is a school of thought promoted by some that there is no real reason for study since God will tell one what to say if he lives close to the Lord. This is pure nonsense. God will not give anyone a Scripture to quote that is not to be found in the Bible. Neither will God give the teacher a thought that is not substantiated by the Bible.

Teachers who become enthused over seeking out Bible truths for themselves will pass this enthusiasm along to those in their classes.

C. Inspired Presentation Is the Teacher's Challenge

The teacher who is truly convinced that the Bible is the inspired, eternal and efficacious Word of the Lord and has diligently applied himself to acquiring knowledge of this Book is most apt to be enthused or inspired when he appears before his class to teach. Lack of conviction on the part of the teacher, as well as failure to study and failure to pray, produces pessimism and indifference in both the teacher and the hearers.

D. Inspired Workers Is the Result

And the things that thou hast heard of me among many witnesses, the same commit thou to faithful men, who shall be able to teach others also (II Timothy 2:2).

The perpetuity of the church until Jesus comes is assured. Jesus Himself declared that the gates of hell would not prevail against it. This continuous succession of true churches is accomplished through the process of one generation teaching the next. Paul reminded Timothy that he was to commit those things he had heard to *faithful* men who would be able to teach others also. Enthused workers and teachers pass both the message and the enthusiasm along to those whom they teach in order that they (the taught) may in turn inspire others to teach.

III. The Teacher Must Present the Lesson in an Interesting Manner

Faithful preparation and inspired presentation will usually result in an interesting class period. Interest among the pupils must be gained and retained throughout the lesson if teaching is to be truly successful. Illustrations, object lessons, gestures, diversity of teaching methods, to name a few approaches, will contribute to interesting teaching. Unless the teacher does command the interest of his pupils there is no point in his teaching at all. The wise teacher will take every precaution to see that all distracting influences are removed, if possible, and he will insist upon every student giving attention to his teaching. But he will not hold the attention of the student long unless he is presenting the lesson in a manner that will attract attention. To do this the teacher must make his teaching interesting.

IV. The Teacher Must Avoid the Seven Success Stealers

As there are some necessary positive attributes for effective teaching, so are there some things to avoid. The wise teacher will be on guard against the seven success stealers.

A. Sensationalism

Sensationalism has been defined as "using effects intended to startle, shock, thrill, or arouse intense excitement."

While it is true that sensationalism may play a role in getting people into the Sunday school class, it is doubtful if it is ever of benefit in the actual teaching of the Word of the Lord. The teacher who is more interested in getting large numbers to attend the class than in feeding those who attend will probably conclude that the end result justifies the means used to get them there. Effective teachers recognize the fact that their responsibility is not primarily to get people to attend. but rather to teach them when they do

PRESENTATION

attend. To startle, shock, thrill, or arouse intense excitement among people is not conclusive proof that they have been properly taught.

We have witnessed much enthusiasm among church members over the prospect of seeing the pastor or the superintendent have a phonograph record broken over his head immediately preceding the worship service. The object of this is to dramatize the fact that a "record was broken" in the Sunday school. We ask, what good is a broken record of attendance if the promotion used to get people to come on that particular day caused those who attended to lose sight of the real reason for being there? Somehow it just doesn't seem in keeping with the solemnity and dignity of church worship to be breaking records over a pastor's head in the sanctuary just before he enters the pulpit to preach!

Other promotional gimmicks just as startling, shocking, and thrilling have been used in order to build attendance. Some of these methods have proven successful for a time but usually when the "gimmicks" are stopped the enthusiasm ceases. It would appear that the work of the Lord must be built around something more substantial.

B. Pharisaism

Pharisaism means "to be self-righteous, sanctimonious, hypocritical."

Possibly this is one of the most deadly of the sins the Christian teacher must guard against. Self-righteousness on the part of a teacher is repulsive because it presents the attitude that the teacher considers himself far better than those whom he teaches. The self-righteous teacher should remember the words of Scripture which declare,

> *All scripture is given by inspiration of God and is profitable ... for reproof, for correction, for instruction in righteousness ...* (II Timothy 3:16).

Nowhere does the Bible admonish the teacher to reprove, correct, or instruct because he, the teacher, is above the need for this himself. Rather, the teacher is to bear in mind that it is the Bible, the Scriptures, which accomplish this work.

Here is another applicable Scripture verse for the self-righteous teacher:

> *Brethren, if a man be overtaken in a fault, ye which are spiritual, restore such an one in the spirit of meekness; considering thyself, lest thou also be tempted. Bear ye one another's burdens, and so fulfil the law of Christ. For if a man think himself to be something, when he is nothing, he deceiveth himself. But let every man prove his own work, and then shall he have rejoicing in himself alone, and not in another. For every man shall bear his own burden. Let him that is taught in the word communicate unto him that teacheth in all good things* (Galations 6:1-6).

Let the self-righteous especially note that those who are spiritual are to *restore the erring one in a spirit of meekness considering himself lest he also be tempted.* This passage of Scripture, as no other, should cause pharisaism to disappear from the scene among those who would teach the Word of the Lord.

A sanctimonious person is one who *pretends* to be very pious—a holier-than-thou attitude. The teacher who would succeed as a teacher will not parade his piousness but rather will recognize his weakness and take his place among those who are earnestly seeking God's will and way.

C. Dogmatism

Dogmatism is "the assertion of opinion, usually without reference to evidence or proof."

It is rather easy for teachers to drift into dogmatism. On any given Sunday morning there is possibly more dogma presented in the class than there is real Bible truth. It is necessary to have opinions in order to teach, but the successful teacher will avail himself of every teaching aid before forming opinions. The assertion of opinion may be interesting but the command to teachers is not to assert opinion but rather the Word of the Lord. Sometimes the differentiation between opinion and fact is difficult. The only way to be sure is to submit opinions to the test of the Word of God. The dogmatic teacher should read prayerfully the admonition of Paul to the Roman Christians:

> *God forbid: yea, let God be true, but every man a liar; as it is written, That thou mightest be justified in thy sayings, and mightest overcome when thou art judged* (Romans 3:4).

D. Negativism

Negativism means "to be characterized by doubt and questions; ignoring or opposing suggestions from others."

The teacher who has any doubts about the Bible being what it claims for itself will never succeed as a teacher. If the Bible cannot be accepted as the inspired, infallible, and eternal Word of God by the prospective teacher he should refuse the work of teaching. To accept the challenge of teaching the Bible while harboring doubts about its validity is blasphemous. This negativism will be transmitted to the students and will do irreparable harm to the teaching ministry.

Surely the church would do well to require of each of her teachers a statement of unqualified acceptance of the Bible as God's inspired message to man. To do less than this is to show too little concern for what is being taught in the classrooms of the church.

The teacher who would be offended by such requirements does not deserve further consideration as a teacher.

To ignore or oppose suggestions from others is a sign of spiritual immaturity. This attitude indicates that the teacher considers himself to have attained the highest knowledge of the subject and has no need that others teach him. Effective teachers have learned that in teaching they sometimes become the pupil and the pupil becomes the teacher! The wise teacher will never ignore the suggestions or expressed thoughts of others.

E. Pessimism

Pessimism is defined as "the practice of looking on the dark side of things, expecting nothing good, expecting the worst."

The teacher who believes that nothing good is going to come from his teaching is usually right! To go into class with the attitude that nothing will be accomplished is to be defeated before the class begins. Just as the minister should expect results from his preaching, so should the teacher confidently expect to witness positive results from his teaching. It will help the teacher who is naturally pessimistic to remember that the power is in the Word of the Lord—not in the teaching of the teacher.

F. Secularism

Secularism on the part of a Christian teacher can become a most fatal practice. Being more concerned with worldly affairs than spiritual values is indeed an attitude against which all successful teachers must constantly be on guard.

Unless the teacher has complete control of the classroom situation, much of the discussion in class is apt to concern worldly affairs. Subjects ranging from parades to politics, space to sports, weather to weddings, and fashions to finances come in for discussion

PRESENTATION

in the classroom if the teacher has a tendency to be secularistic. While all the above mentioned subjects are of importance and should, at the proper place and time, be discussed by the most devout Christians, it is doubtful that the classroom is the appropriate place for discussion except as they are directly related to the lesson under consideration.

The teacher must be spiritually minded. But teachers should learn the difference between being "spiritually minded" and of being "holier-than-thou" or "sanctimonious."

G. Derogativism

Though I failed to find the above word in a dictionary, I believe that it is in order here to "coin" a new one. *Derogativism* (if *you* can't find it in a dictionary) means about the same as "derogation" which means "disparagement, belittling, discrediting, or showing disrespect for."

Surely the Christian teacher will not be guilty of disparaging (attempting to lower in esteem by insinuations or faint praise) the efforts or work of others. The successful teacher has already learned that his success does not come as a result of the demerits of others. No enduring work, including that of teaching, can be established upon the faults and failures of others.

Showing disrespect for others can only lead to a diminishing of one's own respect. This is especially true of the teacher who would show disrespect for the ideas or thoughts of others. The thoughtful, concerned teacher will never ridicule a question or statement of others regardless of how vehemently he may disagree with the position others take.

These are the seven success stealers against which the effective teacher will stand constant guard. To do so is to take a giant step forward toward effective teaching. To fail to do so is to forfeit the faintest hope of successful teaching.